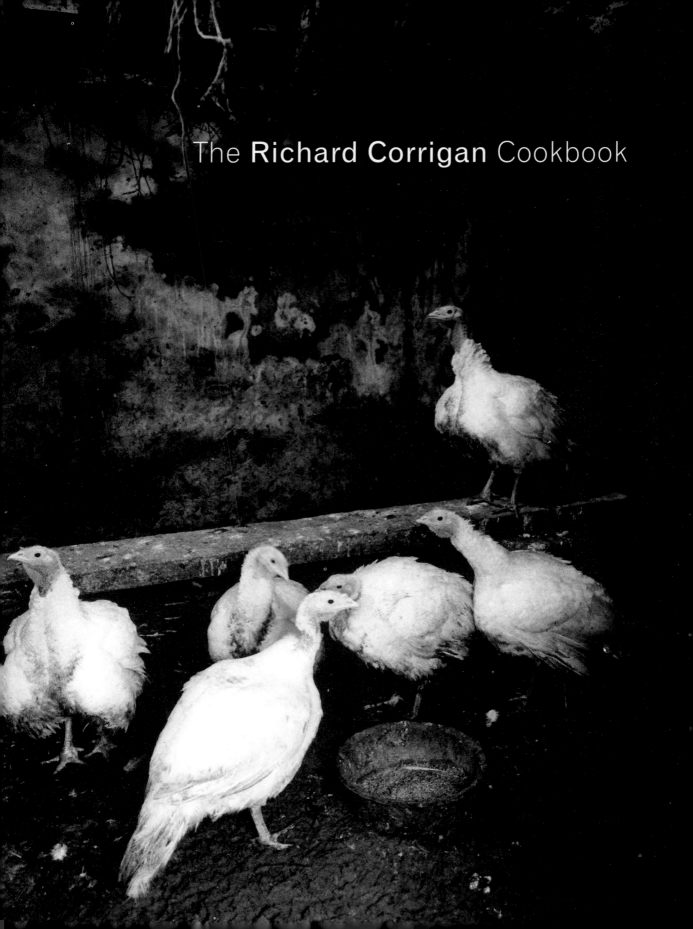

The **Richard Corrigan** Cookbook

THE
richard
corrigan
COOKBOOK

with Norma MacMillan

To Brien,
Life is good.
Richard Corrigan

Photography by **Francesca Yorke**

Hodder & Stoughton

I would like to thank all the staff at Lindsay House, past and present: in particular chef Malcolm Strammer for his help with the photography for this book (after four glorious years working beside me, he now has his own restaurant); chef Gareth O'Brien for his work on the recipes and photography; general manager Thierry Talebon (his Gallic charm and humour were much needed in times of pressure); and Kevin Watson; Douglas Wregg for his wonderful contributions to the wine list at Lindsay House and to this book; Randolph Hodgson for championing British and Irish cheeses and writing about them here; Susanna Tee for testing all the recipes so carefully; Colum Fitzgerald for his enthusiasm and positive criticism (and a brilliant palate); Rick and Nigel Goodhew; Stephen Bull; Matthew Fort; Adrian Gill and Fay Maschler for their support and encouragement; Norma MacMillan for her endless patience with me and her meticulous attention to detail; David Bloomfield for all his work on my behalf; and my wife Maria and my two children, Jessica and Richard, for putting up with me and sticking by me through some difficult times.

Design Alasdair Oliver   photography Francesca Yorke

Extract from 'Clearances' from *New Selected Poems 1966-1987* by Seamus Heaney reprinted by kind permission of Faber and Faber Limited.

First published in Great Britain in 1999 by Hodder and Stoughton
A division of Hodder Headline PLC

The publishers gratefully acknowledge permission to use the excerpts from the W.B. Yeats poems: 'Her Anxiety' on page 19; 'The Wild Swans at Coole' on page 59; 'From the Antigone' on page 106; 'The Lover Tells of the Rose in His Heart' on page 152, with thanks to A.P. Watt on behalf of Michael B. Yeats.

British Library Cataloguing in Publication Data
A CIP catalogue record for this title is available from the British Library

ISBN 0 340 72848 5

Printed and bound in Great Britain by Bath Press

Hodder and Stoughton
A division of Hodder Headline PLC
338 Euston Road
London NW1 3BH

contents

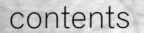

for my mother, Kate Corrigan (1931-1999), who brought
the joyous spirit of her native Connemara to our home

When all the others were away at Mass
I was all hers as we peeled potatoes.
They broke the silence, let fall one by one
Like solder weeping off the soldering iron:
Cold comforts set between us, things to share
Gleaming in a bucket of clean water.
And again let fall. Little pleasant splashes
From each other's work would bring us to our senses.

So while the parish priest at her bedside
Went hammer and tongs at the prayers for the dying
And some were responding and some crying
I remembered her head bent towards my head,
Her breath in mine, our fluent dipping knives —
Never closer the whole rest of our lives.

from **Clearances** by Seamus Heaney

I was born on a farm in County Meath, about two miles from the nearest village. It wasn't a very big farm, only about 25 acres of poor bog land. We lived in a thatched cottage with just four rooms, plus a dairy and larder outside. There were seven of us children. I'm third from the top, which I think is very well placed. We're all very close in age, which made for a tight-knit group when we were growing up.

influences

We were poor – not poor in the sense of what is classed as poverty today, but we were poor. There were no airs and graces in our household. Most of what we ate we grew or killed, shot or poached. My dad is a legend in our area for poaching the salmon. Never caught once. We only poached for the table, not for gain. If you have a family to feed, anything that walks, crawls, swims or flies is fair game. People should not be jailed for putting food on the table, let alone hanged for it, as was once the case. There were huge estates in west Meath. We felt no resentment towards the landowners, but we did take their venison. Country people generally don't like authority, and they don't like people in the city telling them what to do and what not to do.

We had great orchards, planted by my grandfather – cherry trees, apple and pear trees, plums – and we had quite big gardens around the house where we grew cabbages and root vegetables. We always had too many apples – we just picked what we wanted and left the rest for

the birds. Mum made jams and chutneys and she bottled the plums, to be a Sunday dessert. We'd leave the pears on the trees as late as possible and then put them under layers of hay to finish ripening.

There was always a lot of weeding to do. To this day I have nightmares about it. The midges (midgets, we called them) would bite the head off you – they were really lethal in a bog environment. They'd swarm around you, but you'd still have to stay there and weed those drills. If you were told to do something you did it. With so many of us in the house, you had to behave well. There was no room for democracy.

We had chickens, and ducks and geese. I loved the beautiful duck eggs, which the ducks would cover up and hide in corners, quite cleverly. But we knew exactly where to look. The chickens and ducks had to be locked in every night – if one was missing, it would be gone by the morning. The fox would have it.

The neighbours kept our pigs on their farm. After feeding them for the whole year, I'd become very attached to them, but when it came round to September, with the oiling of the gun and the bullets being taken out, I knew that it was 'chop chop' time for my friends. The killing of the pigs was a neighbourly thing because four or five grown men were needed to handle the beasts. Once the pigs were shot, their throats would be cut so the blood could be collected for the black pudding. The men would do all the butchery, and bottles of Guinness would be drunk afterwards, to celebrate. I'd always manage to get my hands on one, and run out the back to drink it. Those were good times.

The pork fillets, which we called grishkeens, would be used fresh – chopped up and fried a week or so later – but the rest, the whole sides, would be salted. We'd eat the joints of bacon boiled, always served with turnips and boiled spuds. The trotters were boiled up too, for crubeens. That would be a delicacy for the men when they came home from the pub. The pigs' heads would be brought to the kitchen, to be boiled, picked and put into an earthenware dish to make brawn, which was absolutely divine. Once cured, the bacon was put down for the winter months, and we'd start rearing two new pigs.

Being country pigs, and because of the way we fed them, they had a huge amount of fat on them. Some of the fat was rendered to make lard, and this was used for frying sausages, rashers or eggs. It was never used for frying anything else. Salty butter, the 'country caviar', was preferred.

One of our great delicacies was eels. These were kept in a big wash tub, punctured with holes, standing in the local river. We'd bring them home, still alive, and mum would chop them up, skin and all, and fry them. I was a devil, though – once I put a live eel in my baby brother's cot!

Living on a farm meant lots of hard work for all of us, particularly in the winter when it got dark very early. We'd be just in from school, have a bite to eat and it would be dark. There'd be 15–18 head of cattle to feed, and bales of hay and straw to shift. I don't remember any relaxation time. There was no feeling of celebration of being on a farm, enjoying your surroundings, as a romantic ideal, although I do now feel nostalgia for things like the call of the pheasants, and hearing the corncrakes and curlews. Few chemicals were thrown on to fields then – farming wasn't intensive, as it is today – so there were always lots of birds and masses of wild flowers in the spring and summer.

When I started school in the local primary I hated it. Coming from a farm, it seemed oppressive. I'd do anything not to go – I would just go walk in the woods and pick hazelnuts. I did everything I could to miss as many days as possible. I'd come back home with my satchel, and sometimes my parents wouldn't know if I'd been at school or not. But after a while I got used to it.

Summer was always a very busy time for us – our school holidays were hard graft. The cutting of the turf was the last job to be done, in August. The slanes were sharpened and we'd all set to work clearing the moss and scrub from the high bank of the bog, to get down to the turf. It was hot, and we'd get very sunburnt. Once the bank was cleared, we'd cut some birch to fill up the holes from the previous year, which were full of water. The bank had to be sharpened up to a proper flat surface so it could be cut down, six or nine layers. My father would cut the turf and we would catch it, all of us children together. We'd put it on the back of a horse and buggy, or tractor and buggy, to take it on to a field to dry. When it was dried out a bit, we'd heap it up into castles to dry and harden some more. After eight weeks the turf was ready to be taken home and stacked up. It was back-breaking work. We'd go back to school feeling pretty tired out.

The turf provided fuel for the fire. It was no good having food hanging up in the barn if you didn't cut your turf, because you'd have no fuel to cook it. The fire also heated the house, which could get very cold and damp in the winter. I still love the smell of smoky peat.

We were brought up with a great sense of values and tradition. The rosary was said in the house every evening, after dinner. And we all went to Mass every Sunday, all turned out in our Sunday best – even the house had to be spick and span. For Sunday lunch we'd always have a rib of beef, collected from the butcher late on Saturday evening. After fatty bacon and cabbage through the week, you'd be happy to see a bit of beef coming in. It was special. Mum would put it in to cook early on Sunday morning. The beef would be medium to well done, and crisp on the outside. The outside was always a prime slice, and my dad usually got it. To this day I still love beef cooked that way.

It was very simple fare for the rest of the week – vegetables and bacon, or sometimes just spuds and butter. And bread. Mum made bread every day – to buy it was shameful. She was a great baker, with strong hands. She'd bake the bread in an open metal casket with cinders of turf under and over it. It's a real art, making bread over an open fire. We made our own butter as well, and got through a pound a day in our house. Churning the butter was a great affair. We all queued up to turn the butter, then used the butter clappers to get the water out. What was left over, the buttermilk, was kept cold and made a delicious drink.

We ate a lot of wild rabbit. My dad would have shot them – we didn't believe in traps or snares because they are very cruel ways to kill an animal – and he would always do the preparation. To see him skinning them was like watching an artist at work. Mature rabbits would be jointed and stewed with onions, carrots, some wild thyme, a bit of wild garlic, salt and water. A sort of pot au feu of rabbit. Potatoes would be on the side, but no veg. With young rabbits, we'd fry the pieces in a big iron pan with just wild thyme and salty butter. Because butter was so plentiful in the country it was always lashed on generously.

Wild salmon was a breakfast treat, cooked simply in our own butter and eaten with brown bread. I'd smell it from my bed and want to rush down to eat it from the pan.

We had to sell our farm in 1976 because we just couldn't make a living from it. The land was too poor. Although I remember feeling sad when the farm was sold, looking back I can't see that it brought any joy to my parents. It was hard work, and often there was no money in the house. Food for the animals sometimes had to come before food on the table.

I can still remember the first meal I had in a restaurant. It was at a small local hotel called the Kirwan Arms where they did weddings and such like. We were all brought there to dinner by my dad as a special treat. I'd have only been 11 or 12. Maybe it was arrogance at a very youthful age, but I felt that I belonged there. And as it happened that was where I got my first job.

I was interested in cooking and felt it might be something I wanted to do. I had always helped my mum with the cooking at home, along with my sisters (I seemed to have a lot of time on my hands, maybe because I never did a bit of homework). I tried to study cooking in the technical school, but they wouldn't accept me because it was considered to be a girly thing then.

So as soon as I finished school, I went to the head chef at the Kirwan Arms, Ray Vaughan, who was a friend of my father, and asked whether there were any jobs going, expecting a 'no'. He said yes, you can start next Monday. I hadn't even told my parents. So I started work, aged about 14. Six months later, I moved out of home to staff accommodation. For the first few weeks I was scrubbing down walls, cleaning cookers, washing up. That's where I started. Then I began working upwards, to peeling spuds and then on to the veg. That was a good thing. After seven or eight months I got on to the starters, which was even better.

Ray was more than kind to me, even when I did crazy things. Everything I messed up he managed to use. It made me realize that nothing is ever over-cooked or under-cooked – nothing is wasted or thrown away in the kitchen, unless it is burnt. You can't get rid of that burnt flavour. Ray put up with me because I was young and keen. He knew that you make mistakes when you are learning. There's so much responsibility placed on you, even as a junior commis.

The owners of the hotel, Sean and Rita Kirwan, wanted to serve the best food locally – not gourmet, but with everything done properly and with really good-quality ingredients. This was long before there was any real interest in good food. It was only a small country hotel after all. They made sure that everything was bought locally. The butcher would come in three times a week, to deliver venison and whole veal carcasses. Ray did all the butchery himself. He was so skilful and quick. Within 15 minutes the joints would be hanging up, and the bones roasting in the oven.

Ray had worked on cruise liners all his life, and everything he prepared was done right, with no shortcuts. For egg mayonnaise, which was big in those days, he made fresh mayonnaise properly, using free-range eggs. Ray ran the place with total discipline. But I had great fun, and Ray always encouraged me. When I told him I was leaving, after two years, to be a commis chef at a new hotel opening in Cavantown, he said you'll be the head chef up there before you know it. I was only 16 or so.

After that, the next job was in the Netherlands. Europe was a different world – to Amsterdam from a small Irish country town! Even so, it didn't faze me to go into a great restaurant kitchen. I had been taught by the best and had worked with the finest and freshest ingredients money can buy, even though it wasn't haute cuisine. In the better restaurants you pick up more skills and techniques, more complicated things and ways to make more sophisticated dishes – you learn the 'high table' of food. It certainly was a great eye-opener to me, a kickstart to acquiring knowledge. I got on very well in the three years I was in the Netherlands. I didn't feel intimidated by the other staff, who were mostly French or German, because once you can cut the mustard in your section you don't have a problem.

From then on it was just the breaks at the time, to London to work in the Meridien Hotel in Piccadilly, and then on to other restaurants in London. I now have my own restaurant, which makes me very proud. It was always my ambition to be my own boss, to cook and serve what I like – after all, the menu is based on my tastes and preferences. There are hard lessons to learn when you run your own establishment – if things go wrong, you can only blame yourself. But it is an achievement, and a privilege.

I think the way I was brought up has made me appreciate the seasons more than most people. On a farm you are always preparing for the next season. At the end of winter you are preparing for spring with the clearing of the land before planting. In spring you plant and, with the days getting longer, see life starting again. Then in summer you are preparing the plants for their harvesting. In autumn you prepare for the winter, killing and salting the pigs, cutting and storing the turf, preserving the potatoes in clay banks in the fields, to keep them fresh late into the winter. It's an endless cycle, and a hard way to live, but when in midwinter you are eating the lovely bottled fruits of summer it seems worth it. You understand then that there was a reason for all the preparation and work.

As a chef, I like the anticipation, the waiting for the foods in season – wild salmon, for example – and then enjoying this king of fish during its time. Nowadays you can go to a restaurant at any time of the year and be served manicured baby vegetables and out-of-season berries. I think this is a lazy opt out. Imported asparagus in March may be good, but I am a purist at heart. Yes, you have to be more creative and innovative if you are cooking food in season, particularly in winter when the choice can be more limited. But salsify and other root vegetables are delicious, and there are always greens to be had. You don't have to rush for the asparagus so early in the season. It will be there soon, to enjoy at its peak.

People go to restaurants now for reasons far removed from eating because they are hungry, or even just enjoying a good meal. It has become more of a fashion statement. I think that's a great disappointment. Respect for food is one of the most important things to have, even if it's for the humblest of vegetables like potatoes, carrots and parsnips. With meat, for example, you need to have respect for the animal it came from, and for the person who made a living from rearing it. It's important to understand the chain of events that brought it to your kitchen.

My approach to food is quite simple really: I tend not to elaborate. I put a few twists here and there, but it's basically very straightforward. You could call it farmhouse cooking with a bit of Cordon Bleu thrown in. I can dish up the fancy stuff if I want to, but I'm just as happy to use the best and freshest ingredients in their season – I love to see simplicity on the plate.

Earth in beauty dressed awaits returning spring

spring

best in spring

cod **plaice** sea trout **herring** mackerel **whitebait** scallops **mussels** hare **rabbit** venison **pigeon** English and Welsh lamb **asparagus** young carrots **turnips** broccoli and sprouting broccoli **cabbages** spring greens **spinach** broad beans **new potatoes** turnips **cucumber** lettuce **wild garlic** gooseberries **rhubarb** pineapple **grapes**

Spring vegetable soup with bacon dumplings

Serves 6

For the dumplings

8 rashers of good unsmoked bacon

olive oil

2 tablespoons finely chopped onion

1 large garlic clove, peeled and
   chopped

2½ tablespoons chopped fresh parsley

2½ tablespoons chopped fresh
   tarragon

For the soup

1.5 litres vegetable stock

small bunch of fresh thyme

olive oil

½ small onion, peeled and chopped

1½ garlic cloves, peeled and chopped

2 medium carrots, peeled and
   neatly chopped

1 celery stick, trimmed and
   neatly chopped

1 medium courgette, neatly chopped

1 small leek, trimmed and
   neatly chopped

freshly ground black pepper

freshly grated Parmesan for serving

First make the dumplings. Cut the rinds off the bacon rashers; reserve the rinds for the soup. Mince the bacon very finely in a food processor – if the bacon is minced too coarsely it will not roll into dumplings and bind properly, and the dumplings will break up. Transfer the bacon to a bowl. Heat a film of oil in a frying pan, add the onion and garlic, and sweat over a low heat until soft but not coloured. Remove from the heat and stir in the parsley and tarragon. Leave to cool, then add to the minced bacon. Season to taste with pepper. Roll the mixture into walnut-sized dumplings, pressing firmly together. Keep, covered, in the fridge until ready to use.

For the soup, put the vegetable stock in a saucepan and add the bacon rinds and thyme. Bring to the boil and simmer for 15 minutes. Strain.

Heat a film of oil in the saucepan, add the onion and garlic, and sauté over a moderate heat for about 2 minutes, stirring frequently. Add the carrots and sauté for 2 minutes. Add the celery and courgette, and sauté for another 2 minutes. Finally, add the leek and sauté for 2 more minutes. Pour the stock into the pan and bring to the boil. Simmer for 7-8 minutes or until the vegetables are just tender but still a little crunchy.

Remove the pan from the heat and add the dumplings. Return to the heat and bring the soup almost to the boil. Simmer gently for 7 minutes.

Check the seasoning, then serve, sprinkled with Parmesan.

I am a great lover of soups, and this vegetable soup with bacon dumplings is my all-time favourite – I love the combination of vegetables and bacon, which is so traditional in Ireland. It is a really uncomplicated soup that can be made very quickly and easily. That is the beauty of it. Give me good, wholesome food, rather than trendy dishes any day.

Although you could make the soup with a stock cube, it is so easy to make your own stock, using the vegetable trimmings.

Cured salmon with shallot, olive oil and lime

Serves 10-12

1.2 kg whole wild salmon fillet
(a side), with skin
coarse sea salt

For the dressing

80 ml extra virgin olive oil
80 ml white wine (Chablis-type)
80 ml freshly squeezed lime juice
50 g caster sugar
100 g shallots, peeled and
finely chopped

2 tablespoons finely chopped
fresh chervil
2 tablespoons finely chopped
fresh chives
1 tablespoon finely chopped fresh dill
salt and freshly ground black pepper

To garnish

very thinly sliced or shaved bulb
fennel dressed with olive oil,
lemon juice and seasoning

It is essential that you use very fresh fish for this, and for me it must be wild salmon, not farmed. Each year I look forward to the wild salmon season with great excitement. Once cured, the salmon will keep 4-5 days in the fridge, and makes a grand dish for a party. Try it with Irish soda bread (see recipe on page 201).

Be sure all the pin bones are removed from the salmon (pull out any remaining with tweezers). Lay the salmon fillet on a tray, skin side down. Sprinkle a light covering of coarse sea salt all over the flesh, then cover with cling film and refrigerate for 6-8 hours.

Rinse off the salt very thoroughly. Immerse the fillet in a bowl of cold water and leave to soak in the refrigerator for 4-5 hours, to be sure that all the salt has been removed.

Meanwhile, make the dressing. Put the oil, wine, lime juice, sugar and shallots in a bowl and mix together until the sugar has dissolved. Cover and set aside. (The dressing can be made the day before and refrigerated; let it return to room temperature before serving.)

Drain the fillet and pat dry with kitchen paper. Slice the salmon with a very sharp knife, cutting diagonally as for smoked salmon, from the direction of the head to the tail.

Arrange the slices on individual plates, spreading them out to cover the plates completely. Season the dressing with salt and pepper, stir well and add the herbs. Spoon the dressing evenly over the salmon. Garnish with the fennel, piled on the salmon in the centre of the plate.

Squid with broad beans and black pudding

Serves 6

8 medium squid (about 500 g),
  cleaned by the fishmonger
olive oil
1 small carrot, peeled and coarsely
  chopped
½ onion, peeled and coarsely chopped
½ bulb fennel, trimmed and coarsely
  chopped
3 garlic cloves, peeled and chopped

good pinch of saffron threads,
  crumbled
1 tablespoon tomato purée
50 ml white wine
115 g shelled fresh young broad beans
  (about 450 g in shell)
½ French horseshoe-shaped black
  pudding (about 225 g)
salt and freshly ground black pepper

Cut the squid bodies into rings and the tentacles in half. Set aside.

Put a generous film of olive oil in the bottom of a large saucepan and set over medium heat. When the oil is hot, add the chopped carrot, onion and fennel, and cook gently for about 5 minutes or until softened, stirring from time to time. Add the garlic and saffron, stir and cover the pan. Lower the heat and cook for 3 minutes.

Add the squid, tomato purée and wine, and stir. Bring to the boil and boil uncovered for 1-2 minutes to evaporate the alcohol. Pour over just enough water to cover and bring back to the boil. Cover the pan again and simmer gently for 40 minutes. About 5 minutes before the cooking time has finished add the broad beans.

Meanwhile, pierce the skin of the black pudding and peel it off. Slice the pudding into 18 equal pieces.

Preheat the oven to 230°C/gas mark 8.

Put a film of olive oil in a baking tin in which the slices of black pudding will fit comfortably, not touching each other. Put the tin in the oven and warm the oil for 1-2 minutes. Arrange the slices of black pudding in the tin and put back into the oven to cook for 6 minutes; they will become quite soft.

Check the seasoning of the squid and bean stew, then ladle it into bowls. With a palette knife, lift the slices of black pudding from the baking tin and place three in each bowl. Serve with crusty bread.

Black pudding takes well to oysters. That is the signature dish of Gerry Galvin of Drimcong restaurant in Galway, and it inspired me to try black pudding with another fish. The result is this dish, which I think is quite delicious.

Soused herring with dill bread

Serves 4

4 plump, spanking fresh herrings,
   scaled, gutted, heads removed
   and filleted

white wine vinegar

Dill Bread (see page 201) for serving

For the souse

120 ml white wine

1 small onion, peeled and thinly sliced

1 carrot, peeled and sliced

2 celery sticks, trimmed and sliced

1 teaspoon dill seed

1 teaspoon mustard seed

2 sprigs of fresh dill, plus
   extra to garnish

piece of bay leaf

1 teaspoon sugar (optional)

sea salt

Immerse the herring fillets in white wine vinegar to cover and leave in a cool place for 4-5 hours. The vinegar will dissolve the majority of the remaining small bones in the fillets. Drain, reserving the vinegar, and pat the fillets dry with kitchen paper. Remove any bones that haven't dissolved.

Combine all the ingredients for the souse, except the sugar, in a large pan and add 360 ml water and 2-3 tablespoons of the vinegar used to soak the herrings. Bring to the boil, then reduce the heat and simmer gently for 35 minutes. Taste to check the seasoning and acidity: you want the mixture to be slightly tart, so add a little more of the reserved vinegar if necessary. Alternatively, if it is too vinegary, add the sugar. Leave to cool.

Pour the cooled souse into a flat dish and slip in the herring fillets. Cover and refrigerate overnight. (The herrings can be kept in the souse for up to 4 days, but no longer.)

Lift the herring fillets out of the souse and slice each in half crossways. Arrange on individual plates with a garnish of a few vegetables from the souse, a spoonful of the liquid to moisten and a fresh sprig of dill. Serve lightly chilled, with dill bread.

Soused fish is a humble dish, but it seems to me more honest than grilled fish with a trendy garnish. It sustained many a fishing family in the coastal towns of Ireland in the last century. Herrings are soft and succulent prepared this way. If you like you can add a garnish of cucumber and plain yogurt or soured cream.

Skate jelly with aubergine and pepper compote

Serves 4-6

1 carrot, peeled

1/2 onion, peeled

6 black peppercorns

1/2 bay leaf

small handful of fresh flat-leaf parsley

4 tablespoons lemon juice

2 skate wings

For the compote

1 large aubergine

sunflower oil

2 red peppers

2 garlic cloves, peeled and sliced

2 small sprigs of fresh thyme

1/2 tablespoon chopped fresh mint

lemon juice

olive oil

salt and freshly ground black pepper

Put the carrot, onion, peppercorns, bay leaf, parsley stalks, lemon juice and 1 litre of water in a large saucepan, big enough to accommodate the skate wings. Add a little salt and pepper. Bring to the boil and simmer for 10 minutes. Strain the stock and return to the pan. Put in the skate wings. They should be just covered with liquid. Cook for 4-5 minutes; do not let the liquid boil.

Remove from the heat and lift the skate wings out of the stock on to a plate. Leave them to cool, covered with a damp cloth. Reserve the stock.

When the skate is cool enough to handle, take the flesh from the bones in neat strips. Layer the strips in a round earthenware dish. Ladle over just enough of the stock to cover the fish. Sprinkle the shredded parsley leaves evenly over the top. Cover with cling film and refrigerate overnight. The stock will set into a jelly. Scoop from the dish to serve.

To make the compote, preheat the oven to 240°C/gas mark 9. Pierce the aubergine all over with a fork, then lay it on a baking tray. Roast for 35-40 minutes or until soft. Remove from the oven and leave to cool.

Meanwhile, heat a little sunflower oil in a cast-iron frying pan that has an ovenproof handle. Put in the whole peppers and cook over high heat, turning to char on all sides. Then add the garlic and thyme and transfer to the oven. Roast for 4-5 minutes. Tip the peppers, garlic, thyme and oil into a bowl, cover with cling film and leave to cool for 20 minutes. Holding the peppers over the bowl to catch the juices, split them in half and peel. Discard the cores and seeds. Cut the pepper flesh into small, neat dice and put into a clean bowl. Strain the juices over the dice.

When the aubergine has cooled, split it in half lengthways and remove the central seeds with a spoon. Scrape the flesh from the skins and place on a chopping board. Sprinkle over the mint, then chop the aubergine flesh finely to a minced texture.

Combine the aubergine and peppers, and season with a squeeze of lemon juice, a dash of olive oil, and salt and pepper to taste. Serve at room temperature.

This is not unlike jellied eels, as it is set with the natural gelatine in the fish bones (or, to be more accurate, cartilage). Make it in the late spring, when we all hope the sun will begin to shine.

Mackerel with sweet potato and lime pickle

Serves 4

4 plump, spanking fresh mackerel,
   filleted

melted unsalted butter

For Malcolm's spice paste

2.5 cm piece of dried tamarind

1 fresh red chilli, split and seeded

2.5 cm piece of fresh ginger, peeled

6 garlic cloves, peeled and
   germ removed

2 tablespoons cumin seeds

seeds from 1 tablespoon
   cardamom pods

1 tablespoon coriander seeds

1 tablespoon fennel seeds

1 tablespoon caraway seeds

1 star anise

1.5 cm piece of cinnamon stick

1/4 teaspoon freshly grated nutmeg

2 teaspoons coarse sea salt

1 teaspoon black peppercorns

150 ml vegetable oil

**For the sweet potato and
  lime pickle**

10 limes

100 g caster sugar

1 kg sweet potatoes, peeled and
   cut into 1.5 cm dice

1 fresh red chilli, seeded and
   finely diced

1 tablespoon chopped fresh coriander

For the raita

1 teaspoon cumin seeds

200 ml Greek yogurt

1 cucumber, peeled, seeded and diced

lemon juice

1 heaped tablespoon finely shredded
   fresh mint

salt and freshly ground black pepper

First make the spice paste. Preheat the oven to 150°C/gas mark 2. Put all the ingredients, except the oil, in a small roasting tin and warm in the oven for 3-5 minutes or just until you can smell the aromas of the spices when you open the oven door. (Do not let the spices brown or they will taste bitter.) Alternatively, if you don't want to turn the oven on, warm the spices in a dry frying pan. Tip all the spices into a blender or food processor and grind to a very fine powder, or use a mortar and pestle or a clean coffee grinder. Add the oil gradually, blending or pounding to make a soft paste that will run off a spoon. Set aside.

    For the pickle, peel the limes, working over a bowl so that you catch all the juice, then separate the segments, cutting between the membranes. Put the lime segments in the bowl and squeeze in all the juice from the membrane. Add the sugar and stir until dissolved. Add 2-3 tablespoons of the spice paste.

    Cook the sweet potato dice in boiling salted water for 3-5 minutes or until just tender; drain. While still warm, add to the lime pickle. Add the red chilli and stir to mix.

This recipe will make more spice paste than you need, but it will keep in the fridge, with a film of oil on the surface, in a tightly covered jar for 2-3 weeks (if you keep it longer than a week, add more ginger and garlic as their flavour will diminish). It has lots of other uses – add a spoonful or two to cooked rice or brush it on to chicken or lamb chops before grilling.

Cover and leave for at least 2 hours, or overnight if possible (in the refrigerator). Before serving, warm the pickle to body heat and stir in the coriander.

To make the raita, warm the cumin seeds in a small pan until you can smell the spice; do not brown. Tip into a bowl and add the yogurt and cucumber. Season with lemon juice, salt and pepper. Just before serving, stir in the mint.

To cook the mackerel, score the skin side of each fillet with three slashes. Brush the skin with melted butter, then brush on a thin coating of the spice paste. Grill, skin side up, under a moderate heat for 2-3 minutes or until just cooked (the flesh furthest from the heat should still be slightly opaque).

Spoon the warm sweet potato and lime pickle on to each plate and set two fillets on top. Top each serving with a spoonful of raita and serve, with the remaining raita in a separate bowl.

Wild salmon wrapped in *lardo* with salsify and fennel emulsion

Serves 4

4 wild salmon steaks (about 150 g
   each), cut from the centre about
   2 cm thick, central bone
   and skin removed
4 strips of very thinly sliced *lardo*
sunflower oil

For the salsify

juice of 1/2 lemon
8 sticks salsify
1-2 garlic cloves, peeled
fresh bouquet garni of thyme and
   bay leaf
30 g unsalted butter

For the green olive paste

1/2 garlic clove, peeled

8 large green olives, preferably
   unbrined, stoned
1-2 tablespoons olive oil
leaves from 3 sprigs of fresh tarragon,
   finely chopped

For the fennel emulsion

unsalted butter
1/2 bulb fennel, chopped and feathery
   part reserved (or use 2 tablespoons
   chopped fresh herb fennel)
1 garlic clove, peeled and chopped
1 shallot, peeled and chopped
150 ml vegetable stock
6 tablespoons double cream
salt and freshly ground black pepper

Be sure all the bones have been removed from the salmon steaks. Wrap a strip of lardo around the outside of each steak, just as you would wrap a tournedos in fat, and tie it on with string. Set aside in the fridge.

To prepare the salsify, half fill a deep saucepan with water and add the lemon juice. Trim and peel the salsify, then cut in half, dropping each stick into the acidulated water as it is prepared (to prevent discoloration). When all the salsify is in the pan, add the garlic and bouquet garni and bring to the boil. Simmer for 5-6 minutes or until the salsify is just tender but still quite firm. Remove from the heat and leave to cool in the liquid. When cool enough to handle, drain and cut into matchsticks 13-15 cm long. Set aside.

For the olive paste, pound the olives and garlic in a mortar with a pestle to a coarse paste consistency. Gradually mix in enough oil to loosen the paste a little, then add the chopped tarragon. Taste and season. Set aside.

Preheat the oven to 230°C/gas mark 8.

To make the fennel emulsion, melt a knob of butter in a saucepan, add the fennel, garlic and shallot, and sweat gently until very soft. Pour in the stock and bring to the boil. Add the cream and stir, then simmer for 3 minutes. Remove from the heat. Purée the mixture in a blender or food processor, then

Here boneless wild salmon steaks are pan-roasted – seared on top of the stove and then put into the oven to finish cooking – which is a very common technique in professional kitchens. If you don't want to turn the oven on just for the salmon you can cook them completely on top of the stove, but take care not to overcook them. *Lardo* is the fat from Parma ham; you can also use the fatty part of Parma ham slices. The refreshing flavour of salsify goes so well with the oiliness of the salmon – it's a pity that this super vegetable isn't more widely used.

press it through a sieve into a clean pan (we sieve the sauce in the restaurant, but it isn't necessary to do this). Add the chopped feathery part of the fennel (or herb fennel) and season with salt and pepper. Set aside.

To cook the salmon, put a film of sunflower oil in a cast-iron frying pan that has an ovenproof handle and set over medium heat. Season the salmon steaks with salt and pepper. When the oil is hot, put the salmon steaks in the pan and sear for about 30 seconds on each side. Transfer the pan to the oven and cook for about 5 minutes (the salmon will be medium rare).

To finish the salsify, melt the butter in a frying pan and toss the salsify to reheat. Season with salt and pepper. Reheat the fennel emulsion, if necessary.

To serve, pile the salsify in the centre of each warmed plate and set a salmon steak on top. Put a small spoonful of olive paste on each steak and spoon the fennel emulsion around. Serve immediately.

Pork cutlet with carrots and courgette chutney

Serves 4

4 pork cutlets, cut 1.5-2 cm thick
(about 225 g each)
12 young carrots with green tops,
preferably organic carrots,
each 17-20 cm long, scraped
and trimmed to leave some
of the green tops
sunflower oil for frying
unsalted butter
sugar
salt and freshly ground black pepper

For the Troisgros courgette chutney

(makes 900 g)

2 small lemons
3 medium courgettes
2 onions, peeled and thinly sliced
100 ml Riesling or other dry white wine
2 teaspoons sugar
24 black peppercorns, coarsely crushed
2.5 cm cube of fresh ginger, peeled
and finely chopped

I use pork cutlets from traditionally reared pigs (I buy from Chessington Farm, which does a mail order service). These have been lightly smoked and cured so they are almost like a bacon chop. Whatever cutlets you use, be sure they are from humanely reared animals.

This fresh chutney is simple yet unusual – a good example of why the Troisgros brothers are so inspiring to chefs and cooks. It can be kept in the fridge for 4-5 days.

For the Troisgros courgette chutney, peel the lemons, cutting away all the white pith, then slice thinly and discard the pips. Cut the courgettes in half lengthways, then across into 2.5 cm pieces.

Combine all the ingredients in a saucepan, adding just a little salt. Cover and cook over a moderate heat for 1 hour, stirring from time to time. At the end of the cooking, there will still be quite a bit of liquid, but once the chutney is cold the consistency will be perfect. Check the seasoning, then leave to cool.

Preheat the oven to 190°C/gas mark 5.

Season the cutlets. Heat a film of oil in a heavy-based frying pan with an ovenproof handle, and fry the cutlets to sear and brown on both sides. Transfer the pan to the oven to finish cooking the cutlets – about 5 minutes.

Meanwhile, put the carrots in a deep-sided frying pan, just cover with boiling water and add a good slice of butter, a good pinch of sugar and salt to taste. Cook gently until tender.

To serve, lift the carrots out of the liquid and arrange on plates with the cutlets. Add a spoonful of chutney to each plate.

Rack of spring lamb with lamb sweetbreads and spiced aubergines

Serves 4

4 racks of lamb (best ends) with
   3 cutlet bones each, chined
plain flour
12 lamb sweetbreads (about 300 g)
2 tablespoons olive oil
1 teaspoon ground cumin
1 garlic clove, peeled and crushed
sunflower oil for shallow frying
For the spiced aubergines
2 aubergines, cut into 1 cm dice
sea salt
4 tablespoons sunflower oil
1 teaspoon ground coriander
1 teaspoon turmeric
1 teaspoon ground cumin

1 teaspoon mustard seeds
1 teaspoon chilli powder
1-2 fresh red chillies, seeded
   and chopped
2.5 cm piece of fresh ginger,
   peeled and chopped
4 garlic cloves, peeled and chopped
150 ml white wine vinegar
60 g light soft brown sugar
salt and freshly ground black pepper
To garnish
4 heaped tablespoons Greek yogurt
cayenne pepper
1 tablespoon chopped fresh coriander

If your butcher has not already done this for you, remove the fat from the racks of lamb, leaving just a thin layer, then cut away all the meat and fat from between the cutlet bones, scraping the bones clean. Set aside.

Remove all the ducts, outer membrane and blood vessels from the sweetbreads, then soak in a bowl of cold water for 2 hours to remove all blood. Drain and dry well.

Mix together the olive oil, cumin and garlic and set aside to infuse for 30 minutes.

To make the spiced aubergine, put the diced aubergine in a colander, sprinkle with salt and leave to drain for 30-45 minutes. Then rinse, squeeze slightly and dry on kitchen paper. Warm a saucepan over a moderate heat, add the oil and, when heated, add the aubergine. Cook gently for 3-4 minutes or until softening but not browned. Add all the spices, the chillies, ginger and garlic, and cook for 2 minutes, stirring well. Pour in the vinegar and bring to the boil, then simmer for 15 minutes. Gradually stir in the sugar, tasting as you go (the mixture should taste piquant, like a chutney). Add salt to taste. Remove from the heat and set aside.

Preheat the oven to 230°C/gas mark 8.

Brush the racks of lamb all over – even the bones – with the flavoured olive oil. Heat a large, heavy frying pan that has an ovenproof handle, or use a flameproof

Sometimes the flavour of lamb is very delicate early in the season – a little garlic and cumin oil help to round out the flavours. If possible, use the new season's English lamb and their sweetbreads, which rival veal in quality at this time of year. Any left-over spiced aubergine is lovely with spiced ham. In the restaurant we mix a little purée of roasted red pepper with the yogurt used to garnish the dish.

casserole. Season the meat of the racks with salt and pepper, then put into the hot pan, bone side down first. Brown and sear well on all sides. Transfer the pan to the oven to finish cooking for 10-15 minutes. When the lamb is cooked to your taste, remove it from the oven and set aside to rest for 5 minutes or so.

Meanwhile, heat a 1 cm layer of sunflower oil in another frying pan. Dust the sweetbreads lightly with flour, then add to the pan and sear all over in the hot oil. Cook until they are browned and crisp on the outside but still moist in the centre.

To serve, carve each rack into 3 cutlets. Put a spoonful of warm spiced aubergine (reheated if necessary) in the centre of each plate and arrange the cutlets round it. Put the sweetbreads between the cutlets. Any juices exuded from the racks of lamb while they were resting can be spooned over the cutlets and sweetbreads. Season the Greek yogurt with salt and cayenne to taste, and stir in the coriander, then put a spoonful on each plate.

Chicken in cream with morels

Serves 4

1 free-range organic chicken (about
    1.5 kg), with giblets if available
plain flour
sunflower oil
175 ml white wine (a sweet vin jaune
    or medium Vouvray are both good)
200 ml double cream
1 garlic clove, peeled and crushed
leaves from a few sprigs of fresh thyme
24 fresh morels, split lengthways and
    washed, or 20 g·dried morels, soaked
    in warm water for 30 minutes to
    rehydrate and then drained
handful of shelled fresh peas (optional)

hot boiled rice for serving

For the stock

1 large onion, peeled and chopped
3 celery sticks, trimmed and chopped
1 carrot, peeled and chopped
1-2 garlic cloves, peeled
few sprigs of fresh thyme
few parsley stalks
small piece of bay leaf
few black peppercorns
chicken stock or water
small piece of chicken stock cube,
    crumbled (optional)
salt and freshly ground black pepper

Joint the chicken into 8 pieces (2 drumsticks, 2 thighs and 4 pieces of breast, 2 of them with wings). Trim off the wingtips and the knuckle ends of the drumsticks and reserve for the stock. Set aside.

I could survive very well on this dish, with a glass of something nice. It's the perfect dish to enjoy with your family.

Put the wingtips, knuckle joints, backbone and giblets (except the liver) in a saucepan and add all the ingredients for the stock, except the stock cube. Cover with chicken stock or water and bring to the boil, skimming well. Simmer for 20 minutes. Remove from the heat and leave to cool for 15 minutes, then strain. Taste and, if necessary, add the stock cube to improve the flavour.

Heat a film of sunflower oil in a large frying pan. Season the chicken joints, then dust them with seasoned flour. Add to the hot oil and fry to a good golden brown on all sides. As the joints brown, remove them to a colander to drain off excess oil.

Heat a heavy, shallow flameproof casserole. Put in the chicken joints, in one layer, and pour in the wine. Bring to the boil and boil to reduce to about one-quarter. Ladle enough stock into the casserole to come half way up the side of the chicken joints. Bring back to the boil, then cover and simmer for 10 minutes.

Add the cream, garlic, thyme and rehydrated dried morels, if using. Season. Leave to simmer, uncovered, for about 15 minutes or until the chicken is cooked through. Remove the chicken joints from the pan and keep warm. Boil the cream sauce for about 10 minutes to reduce. If using fresh morels, add them after 5 minutes of simmering. If using the peas, add them a minute or so after the morels.

Return the chicken joints to the cream sauce. Check the seasoning before serving, with rice.

Young onions with goat's cheese and marjoram

Serves 4

12 young onions

olive oil

200 g soft Irish goat's cheese

1 tablespoon chopped fresh marjoram

2 garlic cloves, peeled and finely
   chopped

cayenne pepper

freshly grated nutmeg

salt and freshly ground black pepper

Preheat the oven to 180°C/gas mark 4.

Trim the roots and green tops from the onions, reserving the green tops. Blanch the onions in boiling salted water for 4-5 minutes, just to soften them. Drain and refresh. Cut each onion in half lengthways.

Arrange the onion halves, cut side up, in a lightly oiled earthenware baking dish. Season with salt and pepper, and drizzle over a little oil just to moisten. Crumble the goat's cheese over the onions, then sprinkle with the marjoram and garlic. Bake for 40 minutes.

Meanwhile, finely slice the reserved green tops.

To finish, sprinkle the green onion tops over the cheese together with a good pinch of cayenne and a little grated nutmeg.

Serve hot.

Young onions about the size of a golf ball – really giant spring onions – are the ones to use for this dish. As you might expect, I use an Irish goat's cheese, the name of which in Gaelic means My Goat. Serve this as a side dish, or as a starter or lunch dish with some good country bread. This is something I'd run to the woods with, to eat on my own!

Fresh broad beans with savory

Serves 4

1.5 kg fresh broad beans
4 tablespoons double cream
1 tablespoon chopped fresh
  summer savory
freshly grated Parmesan
salt and freshly ground black pepper

Remove the beans from their pods. Blanch them in boiling salted water for 1 minute, then drain and refresh. If the beans are any larger than the size of a fingernail, you will need to peel off their skins.

Put the beans in a heavy saucepan, and add the cream, savory and salt and pepper to taste. Heat through, adding a sprinkle of Parmesan just before serving.

I just love the flavour of broad beans, especially when they are young. If you are growing your own beans, plant some savory in front of them and the herb will perfume the beans. Winter savory could be used if summer savory is not available.

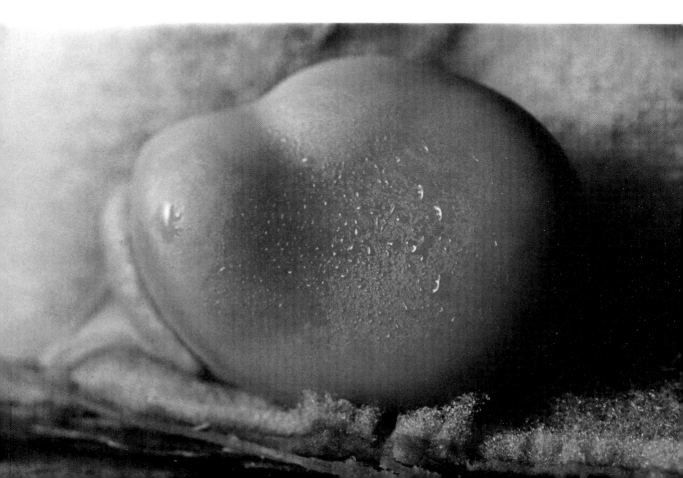

Champn

500 g medium-sized floury potatoes
4-5 spring onions, trimmed and chopped
(white and some of the green)
75 ml double cream or milk
60 g unsalted butter
salt and freshly ground black pepper

Put the unpeeled potatoes into a pan of salted water, bring to the boil and simmer for 20-25 minutes or until tender. Drain and return to the empty pan, off the heat. Cover with a tea towel (or newspaper) and leave to steam and dry off for 5 minutes. Then uncover and leave until cool enough to handle.

Peel the potatoes and put them through a mouli-légumes or potato ricer into a clean saucepan. Set aside.

Put the spring onions and cream in a saucepan and simmer for 1-2 minutes or until the onions start to soften. Mix into the potatoes. Add the butter and season with salt and pepper. Reheat gently, beating until smoothly blended. Serve immediately.

Crème brûlée with blood orange and wholemeal tuile

Serves 6-8

500 ml double cream

1 vanilla pod, split open

grated zest of 1 large orange

6 large egg yolks

about 200 g caster sugar

To serve

4 blood oranges

Wholemeal tuiles (see page 205)

Pour the cream into a heavy-based saucepan. Scrape the tiny seeds out of the vanilla pod into the cream, then add the pod too, together with the orange zest. Heat until bubbles start to form round the edge of the pan, then remove from the heat, cover the pan and set aside to infuse for 20 minutes.

Meanwhile, whisk the egg yolks with 70 g of the sugar until thick and a pale lemon colour.

Pour the hot cream mixture into the yolks, stirring to mix. Return the mixture to the saucepan. Set over a low heat and cook, stirring constantly, for 5-10 minutes or until thickened – you should be able to run your finger across the custard on the back of the spoon and leave a clear trail – and bubbles just start to appear round the edge of the pan. Do not allow the custard to boil. (If you have an instant-read thermometer, you can check to be sure the custard has reached a temperature high enough to kill any bacteria that might be present in the eggs – 81°C.)

Immediately remove from the heat and strain the custard into a jug, pressing all the vanilla seeds through the sieve. Divide the custard among 6-8 ramekins. Allow to cool, then cover and chill overnight to set.

Peel the oranges and cut out the segments from the surrounding membrane. Set the segments aside.

About 30 minutes before serving, sprinkle the remaining sugar over the custard (1 tablespoon to each ramekin), spreading it gently with your finger to make an even layer. Using a blowtorch, melt the sugar and caramelize it to a rich golden brown. Keep the flame moving, as the sugar will bubble up and then change colour. Leave to cool and set.

Set a ramekin on each plate and arrange the orange segments next to it. Add a tuile or two to each plate and serve.

This has a wonderful unctuous texture, quite different from that of a crème brûlée baked in a bain marie. When blood oranges are not available, you can use ruby or pink grapefruit, or even a mixture of citrus, to give a tart contrast to the rich cream.

Pineapple with spiced bread

1 large, perfectly ripe, sweet pineapple
Vanilla ice-cream for serving
(see page 202)
For the spiced bread
250 g clear honey, such as acacia
125 g light soft brown sugar
75 g unsalted butter
225 g plain flour
1 1/2 tablespoons baking powder

1 teaspoon ground ginger
1 teaspoon ground cinnamon
1 teaspoon freshly grated nutmeg
1/4 teaspoon ground cloves
1/2 teaspoon ground allspice
50 g flaked almonds
50 g raisins, chopped
grated zest of 1 lemon
grated zest of 1 orange

You could serve this to four people, using a small pineapple, which will mean you will have more spiced bread than you need. But that is no hardship – it is delicious plain with a cup of tea or coffee, or you can use it to make the spiced bread ice-cream on page 202

Preheat the oven to 180°C/gas mark 4.

For the spiced bread, put the honey, sugar and butter in a saucepan and add 200 ml water. Bring to the boil, stirring to dissolve the sugar. When the mixture is smooth and the butter has melted, remove from the heat and cool to lukewarm. Sift the flour, baking powder and all the spices into a bowl. Add the syrup and stir to mix well. Add the almonds, raisins and zests. Pour the mixture into a 1.7 litre loaf tin lined with greaseproof paper. Bake for 45-60 minutes or until a skewer inserted into the centre comes out clean.

Cool in the tin.

When ready to serve, turn the spiced bread out of the tin and cut 2.5 cm slices. Peel the pineapple, cutting out all the 'eyes', then cut across into 8-10 finger-thick slices. Stamp out the core from the centre of each slice using a small ring cutter.

To serve, put a slice of spiced bread on each plate and top with a ring of pineapple. Add a quenelle of vanilla ice-cream to each plate.

dessert | spring | 49

Banana tart with raisin syrup and rum cream

Serves 8

500 g fresh puff pastry
8 small, ripe but firm bananas
very soft unsalted butter
icing sugar
For the raisin syrup
40 g sultanas
170 g sugar
2 tablespoons dark rum
For the frangipane
100 g caster sugar

100 g unsalted butter,
  at room temperature
1 egg + 1 egg yolk
100 g ground almonds
20 g plain flour
For the rum cream
300 ml double cream
1 tablespoon icing sugar
2 tablespoons dark rum

For the raisin syrup, put the sultanas into a small saucepan, cover with water and bring to the boil. Remove from the heat and leave to soak overnight to plump up. Drain and set aside.

Roll out the puff pastry until very thin (about 3 mm). Cut out 13 cm discs and set them on baking trays lined with greaseproof paper. Using your thumb and index finger and the back, blunt edge of a knife, crimp the edge of each disc to make a rim. Prick the centre of each disc all over with a fork. Set aside in the fridge to rest for 20-30 minutes.

To make the frangipane, cream the butter with the sugar using an electric mixer until pale and fluffy. Lightly beat the egg with the egg yolk, then gradually add to the creamed mixture, beating. Fold in the almonds and flour until well mixed.

Preheat the oven to 200°C/gas mark 6.

Spoon the frangipane on to the centre of the pastry discs and spread out to make a mound about 6 mm thick, leaving 1.5 cm of the pastry uncovered all round. Thinly slice each banana, keeping the slices together. Reserve about 6 slices, then fan out the remainder around the frangipane, leaning them on to it slightly and curving all the way round. The slices should be closely overlapping. Cover the top of the frangipane with the reserved banana slices. Brush the banana with soft butter.

Dust the banana slices generously with icing sugar, then bake the tarts for about 20 minutes or until the bananas are caramelized and shiny and the pastry rim is puffed and golden.

While the tarts are baking, finish the raisin syrup. Gently melt the sugar in a heavy-based pan, then cook until it caramelizes to a light golden brown. Carefully add the

The butter for brushing over the banana slices must be very soft, but not melted as that would not give a thick enough coating. If not cooking immediately, cover the tarts with cling film and keep in the fridge; the bananas may discolour a bit, but don't worry, they will still bake to an appetizing golden brown.

rum, stirring constantly to blend, then stir in the sultanas. Keep hot.

For the rum cream, whip the cream until starting to thicken. Sweeten with sugar to taste and add the rum. Continue whipping until thick.

To serve, set a tart in the centre of each plate. Drizzle round the raisin syrup and add a quenelle or dollop of rum cream.

Chocolate and burnt almond ice-cream

Serves 6

For the almond praline
60 g shelled unblanched almonds
60 g granulated sugar
For the ice-cream
225 g granulated sugar
2 teaspoons instant coffee powder
or granules

225 g bitter chocolate, preferably
Valrhona or a good Belgian
chocolate, broken into small pieces
450 ml double cream
1 tablespoon icing sugar
1/2 teaspoon pure vanilla extract

To make the praline, put the almonds and sugar in a heavy-based saucepan. Cook over a medium-low heat until the sugar has melted, stirring frequently. Continue cooking, stirring occasionally, until the sugar syrup has turned to a deep golden-brown caramel. The almonds will make a popping noise, which indicates that they are toasted.

This fabulously rich ice-cream is based on a sugar syrup, like a sorbet, rather than an egg custard.

Pour the mixture on to a lightly oiled marble slab or baking tray. Spread out so the nuts are in a single layer. Leave to cool and set. When the praline is completely cold, crack it into pieces and put into a strong polythene bag. Coarsely crush with a rolling pin. Set aside.

For the ice-cream, put the granulated sugar and 125 ml water in a heavy-based saucepan and heat, stirring to dissolve the sugar. Bring to the boil. Stir in the coffee until dissolved. Remove from the heat. Add the chocolate to the coffee syrup and stir until melted. Leave to cool, stirring now and then to be sure it remains smooth.

Whip the cream until thick. Add the icing sugar and vanilla extract, and whip until the cream is thick again. Fold into the chocolate mixture followed by the praline. Pour into an ice-cream machine and freeze. Once softly frozen, transfer to a freezerproof container and put into the freezer to 'mature' for an hour or so. If freezing for longer than 1 hour, transfer the ice-cream to the fridge 20 minutes before serving to soften slightly.

Stewed rhubarb with ginger and crème anglaise

700 g forced rhubarb, trimmed and
cut into 3 cm pieces
50 g piece of fresh ginger,
peeled and sliced
300 g sugar
1 tablespoon grenadine

Serves 6
To serve
Crème anglaise (see page 202),
made with milk and cream
but without vanilla
Brittany sablés (see page 205)

Tender forced rhubarb appears in the markets at the end of winter, and I am always glad to see it. I think it is best prepared very simply so that its flavour can be appreciated. If you make this later in the year, you will need to peel the rhubarb. The grenadine is just a bit of a cheat to improve the colour of the syrup.

Spread out the rhubarb in a wide-bottomed pan, such as a clean, heavy-based roasting tin. If possible, the rhubarb pieces should be in a single layer; this will make them less likely to break up when cooked. Scatter the ginger slices over the rhubarb.

Put the sugar into a saucepan and add 300 ml water. Bring to the boil, stirring to dissolve the sugar. Pour enough of this hot syrup over the rhubarb just to cover the fruit. Set the pan of fruit on a moderate heat. Bring the syrup back to boiling point, but don't allow it to bubble up. Poach gently for 3-5 minutes or until the rhubarb is just beginning to soften; test with the point of a sharp knife. Remove the pan from the heat and leave the rhubarb to cool in the syrup.

Discard the ginger, then spoon the rhubarb and syrup into soup plates. Serve with the hot crème anglaise and sablés.

Spring wine

Many of the criteria for recommending wines to go with food are connected to an understanding of the French notion of *terroir*. On the physical side, terroir refers to the interrelationship between the micro-climate of a vineyard, the composition of the soil and the local agriculture, all of which contribute to the flavour of the wine. But the word terroir has deeper connotations, such as the notion of respect for tradition, culture and family, respect for practices handed down the century and, most importantly, a sense of affinity with, and respect for, the land and the changing of the seasons.

Spring witnesses a mood change from cold to warm, from heavy to light and from dark to bright, posing an opportunity to experience new aromas and sensations and to reinvigorate palates accustomed to a diet of powerful winter red wines. Matching wine and food is an intuitive exercise based upon our individual taste preferences and also on our moods, which are, in turn, determined by factors as various as the fickleness of our maritime climate and the way we feel on a given day. We respond instinctively to the cycles of nature. Thus, as the sap rises in the vine, the bud breaks and flowering begins, we tend to feel like drinking sappy, floral wines. Think of that youthful vibrancy in new vintages of Sauvignon Blanc from the Loire valley: of minerally Menetou-Salon, or Sancerre with its exuberant, sometimes grassy-green crunchiness and gooseberry fruit. These wines remind us of fresh lettuce pulled from the ground, herbs and currant leaves, peas, broad beans and asparagus.

Spring may also suggest a racy Chablis, an ideal companion to shellfish, especially oysters. Cured and naturally oily fish (such as mackerel) invite smoky whites with penetrating acidity, whilst soused herrings and fish marinated in oil and lemon juice work against complex wines. With them, try a green-white wine with the sea in its roots, so to speak, such as a pungent Verdejo from Rueda or a Vinho Verde, a gum-tingling Gros Plant from the Pays Nantais, a lip-smacking iodine-edged Picpoul from Bouzygues or, alternatively, salty Manzanilla or dry Amontillado from Jerez. Or, failing all that, take Hugh Johnson's recommendation of Guinness!

Graze on new season's reds with light meats. Pork, chicken and the new season's lamb attract a warm gravelly Bourgeuil or Chinon or a medium-bodied Rhone brimming with young peppery Syrah fruit and fugitive aromas of thyme and marjoram. A purple-fruited Spanish Garnacha from Navarra would equally fit the bill, as would a charming Savigny-les-Beaune with its wonderfully delicate perfume of meadow flowers.

Douglas Wregg

Spring cheese

Variability is one of the most intriguing things about farm cheeses. Cheesemaking, like winemaking, is a fermentation process, and the cheesemaker never has complete control of the fermentation. Unlike wine, however, which has a vintage once a year, cheese is made daily so, in effect, there is a 'vintage' every day.

A lot has been written about the quality of cheese made on the first spring flush of grass. This may be true of cheeses made from the milk of animals grazing on alpine pastures, but in most places (Britain and Ireland included) the spring flush of grass often means thin milk with low proteins and fats, and results in poor cheese. Certainly in the first week the animals actually go out to grass their metabolism is upset, and cheese made from their milk can be very uncertain.

As a rough guide the most reliable cheeses made in spring are the soft sheep's milk cheeses:

Emlett
Little Ryding
Flower Marie

These are all at perfection within a few weeks of making, so the eating season is spring too.

Randolph Hodgson, Neal's Yard Dairy

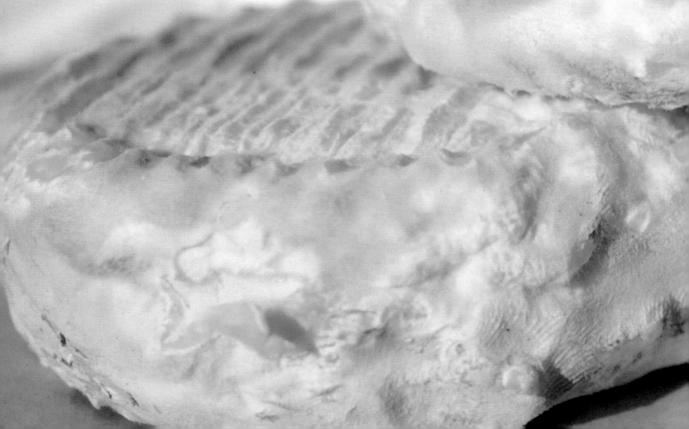

the water mirrors a still sky

summer

best in summer

dover sole **plaice** haddock **salmon** mackerel **lobster** crab **prawns** hare **rabbit** venison **grouse** pigeon **quail** asparagus **peas** broad beans **sweetcorn** runner beans **French beans** vegetable marrow **salad greens** tomatoes **radishes** spring onions **apricots** peaches **nectarines** berries **currants** cherries **dessert gooseberries** plums **melon** elderflowers

Lobster with potato, anchovy and broad bean salad

Serves 4

150 g podded fresh young broad beans
(about 350 g in pods)
250 g small new potatoes, scrubbed
2 live lobsters (each about 450 g)
100 ml extra virgin olive oil
2 1/2 tablespoons lemon juice

4 tablespoons coarsely chopped
fresh flat-leaf parsley
8 'freshly cured' anchovy fillets (sold in
refrigerated deli counters)
salt and freshly ground black pepper

You must eat this on the day of making, as the freshness of the simple ingredients would be spoiled if the dish were refrigerated. I prefer lobster undercooked – not raw, like sushi, but just becoming opaque, when it is still very moist and juicy.

Blanch the broad beans in boiling salted water for 4-5 minutes. Drain and refresh, then, if they are not very small and tender, gently squeeze each bean out of its skin. Set aside.

Add the potatoes to a saucepan of boiling salted water and cook for 15-20 minutes or until just tender.

Meanwhile, put the lobsters into another large pan of boiling salted water and clamp on the lid quickly. When the water comes back to the boil, boil for 5 minutes. Remove the lobsters and refresh under cold running water to stop the cooking (this will keep the meat moist). Crack open the shells with the help of a sharp knife and remove the lobster meat, in whole pieces if possible. Mix together the oil and lemon juice, and drizzle a little of this dressing over the lobster to keep the meat succulent. Set aside.

When the potatoes are cooked, drain well. Return to the hot pan, cover with a tea towel (or newspaper) and leave to dry a bit. As soon as they are cool enough to handle, slice them thickly. Mix with the beans and toss gently with the remaining dressing. Fold in the parsley and season with salt and pepper.

Pile the potato and bean salad in the centre of the plates. Slice the lobster body shell meat into neat discs and arrange on the salad. Add the claw meat to each plate, in whole pieces. Set the anchovy fillets on top and serve.

Fresh pea and scallop soup

Serves 6

1 celery stick, trimmed and diced

1/2 onion, peeled and diced

1/2 leek, trimmed and diced

1 garlic clove, peeled and crushed

30 g unsalted butter

1 tablespoon plain flour

1 litre chicken or vegetable stock,
   heated to boiling

450 g podded young fresh peas
   (about 1 kg in pods)

1 tablespoon each coarsely chopped
   fresh parsley, chives and mint

12-18 small fresh scallops, or 24-30
   queen scallops, removed from shells

salt and freshly ground black pepper

crème fraîche to garnish

Sweat the celery, onion, leek and garlic in the butter until soft but not coloured. Add the flour and stir in well, then pour in the stock, stirring. Bring to the boil, then reduce the heat and simmer for 10 minutes. Strain the stock and leave to cool completely.

Meanwhile, add the peas to a pan of boiling salted water, bring back to the boil and boil for 1 minute. Drain and refresh with cold water, then leave to cool completely.

Add the peas to the cold stock with two-thirds of the mixed herbs. Purée in a blender or food processor. Pour into a saucepan and heat to just below boiling. Check the seasoning.

Remove all grit from the scallops. If using larger scallops, cut each one vertically in half; leave queenies whole. Add the scallops to the hot soup and cook for 40-50 seconds, just until the scallops turn opaque.

Ladle into soup plates and garnish each serving with a spoonful of crème fraîche and a sprinkling of the remaining herbs.

This is beautifully green, just like the Emerald Isle. It is a very simple soup, yet quite delicious. Combined with the fresh scallops it is heavenly.

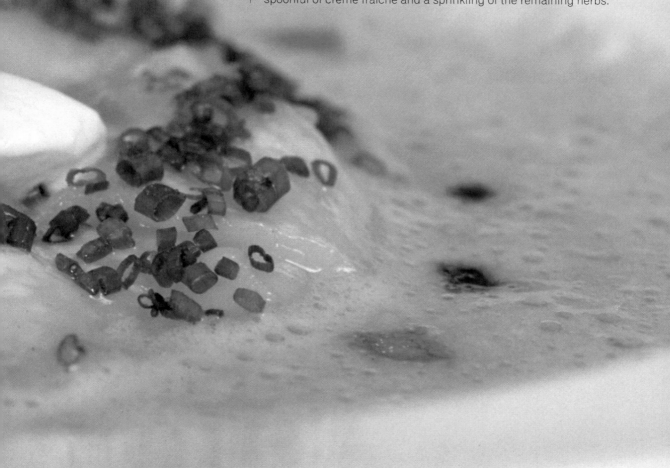

Pike and eel pâté

Serves 8-10

300 g eel fillet from the top end, 20 cm
   long, skinned and cut into 4 strips
3½ tablespoons chopped fresh parsley
2 tablespoons chopped fresh tarragon
2 tablespoons chopped fresh chives
2 tablespoons chopped fresh chervil
25 g button mushrooms,
   finely chopped
4 tablespoons dry white wine
650 g pike, filleted and skinned

2 large egg whites
2 teaspoons brandy
375 ml double cream, well chilled
¼ teaspoon cayenne pepper
40 g fresh white breadcrumbs

For the sauce
250 ml double cream
lemon juice
2 tablespoons Dijon mustard
salt and freshly ground black pepper

Put the strips of eel fillet in a shallow dish. In a bowl mix together 2 tablespoons of the parsley, 1½ tablespoons of the tarragon, all of the chives and chervil, the mushrooms, wine and some salt and pepper. Pour this mixture over the eel fillets and turn them to coat, then leave to marinate for 2 hours.

Tip the eels and marinade into a pan and bring to the boil. Reduce the heat and simmer gently for 10 minutes. Remove from the heat and leave to cool, then chill well.

Put the pike fillet in the bowl of a food processor, cover and chill for 30 minutes. Set the bowl on the processor base and process the fish to make a very fine purée. With the machine running, slowly add the egg whites through the feed tube. Add 1½ teaspoons salt and the brandy, then slowly add the chilled cream and cayenne.

Preheat the oven to 180°C/gas mark 4.

Mix the breadcrumbs with the remaining parsley and tarragon. Add 5 teaspoons of the liquid marinade from the eel fillets and stir to moisten the crumbs.

Put half of the pike mixture into a buttered 1.5 litre terrine mould and smooth into an even layer. Top with a layer of half of the breadcrumb mixture. Arrange the eel fillets on top, placing them lengthways in the mould. Add the remaining breadcrumb mixture, then top with the rest of the pike mixture, smoothing it over.

Cover the mould with foil and set in a large roasting tin of hot water (bain marie). Poach in the oven for about 40 minutes. The pâté is cooked when a skewer inserted into the centre comes out clean. Remove from the bain marie and leave to cool to room temperature.

To make the sauce, pour the juices from the mould into a small bowl and stir in the cream, mustard and a squeeze of lemon juice. Turn out the pâté and cut into neat slices. Serve with the sauce. A beetroot and onion salad would be a lovely garnish.

This puts me in mind of the Ted Hughes poem *Pike*: "…Suddenly there were two. Finally one/With a sag belly and the grin it was born with." The recipe takes a bit of time and effort to prepare, but it's worth it. Dill bread (see recipe on page 201) is very good with it.

Salad of Cornish crab with globe artichoke

Serves 4

1 live Cornish crab (about 1.4 kg)

large wedge of lemon

1 bay leaf

1 garlic clove, peeled and crushed

a few sprigs of fresh thyme

4 medium globe artichokes

2 tablespoons fresh mayonnaise (optional)

For the vinaigrette

6 tablespoons best olive oil

2 tablespoons lemon juice

1 teaspoon Dijon mustard

2 eggs, hard-boiled

1 tablespoon finely chopped fresh parsley

salt and freshly ground black pepper

Drop the crab into a pot of boiling salted water. Bring back to the boil and simmer for 15-20 minutes. Drain and rinse in cold water. Set aside to cool while you prepare the artichokes.

Put 1 litre of water in a saucepan and squeeze in the juice of the lemon wedge. Add the squeezed wedge to the pan together with the bay leaf, garlic and thyme plus some salt and pepper. Cut off the stalk and remove all the leaves from the artichokes until just the meaty heart remains. As each artichoke heart is prepared, drop it into the pan of flavoured water (this will prevent the artichoke from turning black). When all the artichokes are in the pan, cover with a piece of greaseproof paper and place a small plate or saucer on top to keep them submerged. Bring to the boil, then reduce the heat and simmer for 15-20 minutes or until tender (test with the tip of a sharp knife). Remove from the heat and leave to cool in the liquid.

To make the vinaigrette, whisk together the oil, lemon juice, mustard and seasoning to taste in a small bowl. Set aside. Shell the eggs and separate the yolks from the whites. Grate the yolks and whites separately. Set aside.

Crack open the crab and remove all the meat from the body and legs (discard the gills or 'dead men's fingers'). Pick over the meat to be sure there are no bits of shell or cartilage. Put all the meat in a bowl and season to taste. Lightly mix the brown and white meat together. If you like, bind the crabmeat with the mayonnaise.

Drain the artichoke hearts and scoop out the hairy choke from the centre. Slice each heart on the diagonal. Season and dress with a little of the vinaigrette.

To serve, make a pile of crabmeat in the centre of each plate. Surround with the artichoke slices, leaning them against the crabmeat. Add the grated egg (both yolk and white) and parsley to the remaining vinaigrette and spoon round the crab.

The best crabs come from the milder waters of southern England, and the best way to enjoy them is in a simple, unmucked-around preparation.

This salad of crab and artichoke is absolutely delicious.

Rabbit terrine with prunes and marc de bourgogne

Serves 10-12

1 small plump rabbit
2 pig's trotters or 5 leaves of gelatine
3 carrots, peeled
4-5 celery sticks, trimmed and halved
1 onion, peeled and halved
2 garlic cloves, peeled
6 black peppercorns, coarsely crushed
1 bay leaf

a few sprigs of fresh thyme
1 tablespoon marc de bourgogne
walnut oil
12 Agen prunes, stoned and rehydrated
   in tea if not ready-to-eat
coarse sea salt to finish
salt and freshly ground black pepper

Put the rabbit in a pot with the pig's trotters, if using, the vegetables, garlic, peppercorns and herbs. Cover generously with water. Put a sheet of greaseproof paper over the top of the pot and then the lid to make a good seal. Bring to the boil, then reduce the heat and simmer for 40-45 minutes or until the rabbit is cooked through and tender.

You could garnish each serving of this terrine with a little green salad tossed with some walnuts.

Remove the rabbit to a tray, cover with a damp cloth to keep it moist and set aside to cool. Strain the stock into a clean pan, reserving the vegetables in the sieve (discard the pig's trotters and flavourings). Bring the stock back to the boil and boil to reduce by about half, to 800 ml, skimming as necessary. Remove from the heat and add the marc de bourgogne. Taste the stock to check the seasoning. Strain the stock through muslin into a bowl. If you haven't used the pig's trotters (which will make the stock jelly when it has cooled), you will need to set it with the gelatine. Soak the leaves in a little cold water until softened, then drain and add to the hot stock. Stir until the gelatine has melted completely. Set the stock aside to cool (but not until set).

Meanwhile, take the meat from the rabbit, which will still be slightly warm, keeping it in large pieces (discard the offal). Put the pieces of meat back on the tray. Cut the carrots lengthways into quarters, and split the celery sticks lengthways in half. Discard any hard outer layers from the onion, then separate the rest into layers. Add all the vegetables to the tray. Season the rabbit and vegetables with salt and pepper. Sprinkle the rabbit with about 2 teaspoons of walnut oil and leave to absorb for a few minutes.

In a terrine mould or earthenware dish (round or oval) of about 1.5 litre capacity, layer half of the rabbit and vegetables. Turn the prunes in the juices on the tray, then arrange in a layer in the mould. Cover with the rest of the rabbit and vegetables. Ladle in enough of the stock almost to fill the mould. Chill until starting to set, then check to be sure all the rabbit and vegetables are submerged; add another ladleful of stock if necessary. Return to the fridge to set completely.

When ready to serve, turn the terrine out of the mould and cut into slices. Arrange the slices on plates, and finish with a drizzle of walnut oil and a sprinkling of coarse sea salt.

Bavarois of beetroot with smoked eel

Serves 6

6 medium-sized fresh beetroots
5 tablespoons good red wine vinegar
3 leaves of gelatine
250 ml whipping cream
1/2 tablespoon raspberry vinegar

freshly grated horseradish
250 g smoked eel, thinly sliced
salt and freshly ground black pepper
watercress to garnish

This is a good dish to persuade those who don't like beetroot to try it. Fresh horseradish perfumes the whole bavarois – you only need a tiny bit as it is very pungent. We get our smoked eels from Bill's Eels in Norfolk.

Preheat the oven to 180°C/gas mark 4. Scrub the beetroots gently, but do not trim them. Wrap in foil and put on a baking tray. Bake for 1½-2 hours or until tender.

Meanwhile, boil the red wine vinegar for about 1 minute to reduce by half. Leave to cool.

Unwrap the beetroots and leave until they are cool enough to handle, then peel and chop coarsely. Put into a food processor with the reduced vinegar and blend to a smooth purée. Season to taste with salt and pepper. Tip the beetroot purée into muslin-lined sieve set over a bowl. Leave to drain for 2-3 hours.

Break off ¼ of a leaf of gelatine and reserve; soak all the remaining gelatine in 2 tablespoons cold water until softened. Gently warm the beetroot purée (reserve the juice that has drained out into the bowl). Remove the gelatine from the water, add to the purée and stir until completely melted. Turn into a bowl and chill for 5 minutes (not until set).

Meanwhile, whip the cream until thick and a soft peak will form. Fold the cream and the raspberry vinegar into the beetroot purée. Set 6 metal rings, each about 11 cm diameter and 5 cm deep, on a tray. Divide the beetroot mixture among the rings; it should not fill them completely. Chill until set.

Soften the reserved ¼ leaf of gelatine as before. Warm the beetroot juice drained from the purée, then stir in the gelatine.

Sprinkle the top of each set beetroot bavarois with freshly grated horseradish – a tiny bit or more, to taste. Spoon over the beetroot juice, then chill again to set.

To serve, transfer each bavarois to a plate with the help of a slotted spatula. Loosen the bavarois from the metal ring using a knife, then lift off the ring. Arrange the smoked eel round the bavarois and garnish with watercress.

Whiting pan-roasted, with spring cabbage and caper-lemon butter

Serves 4

2 Hisby cabbages or $^1/_2$ Savoy cabbage,
    finely shredded
2 whitings (450 g each), filleted and
    each fillet halved widthways
softened unsalted butter
sunflower oil
$^1/_4$ teaspoon chopped fresh tarragon

For the caper-lemon butter
1 lemon
80 g unsalted butter
4 teaspoons capers (small ones packed
    in vinegar)
$^1/_2$ tablespoon meat jelly (optional)
salt and freshly ground black pepper

Preheat the oven to 240°C/gas mark 9.

Add the cabbage to a pan of boiling salted water. Bring back to the boil and blanch for 2 minutes, then drain and refresh in cold water. Set aside.

To make the caper-lemon butter, peel and segment the lemon, reserving the juices. Melt the butter in a small pan, then cook until it is hazelnut-brown in colour. Add the lemon segments and juice and the capers, then season with salt and pepper. If you have any meat jelly in the fridge, add ½ tablespoon to finish. Keep warm.

Make sure the whiting fillets are dry, then spread softened butter over the skin side. Generously season both sides. Take a frying pan with an ovenproof handle, large enough to hold all 4 fillets comfortably, and heat a generous film of oil for shallow frying. When the oil is hot (but not smoking), put in the fillets, buttered side down. Turn down the heat and cook until the skin crisps nicely, then turn the fillets over on to the flesh side to sear for 1½ minutes. Turn the fillets back over on to the skin side again. Transfer the pan to the oven to cook for 5 minutes.

Meanwhile, melt a small knob of butter in a pan, add the cabbage and toss to coat. When the cabbage is hot, add the tarragon and seasoning and toss again.

To serve, pile the cabbage on hot plates, top with the whiting fillets and spoon over the sauce.

This is a good way to cook whiting, which is a relatively cheap fish. The method of pan-roasting can be used for many other fish fillets too. Whatever fish you use, be sure that it is absolutely fresh.

Sea bass with asparagus and clam vinaigrette

Serves 4

2 sea bass (about 550 g each), filleted
softened unsalted butter
sunflower oil
16 asparagus spears, stalks peeled

For the clam vinaigrette

1 kg palourde clams (very small ones,
  with teaspoon-sized shells)
1 very small onion, peeled and finely
  chopped
2 garlic cloves, peeled and finely
  chopped

olive oil
170 g potato, cooked, peeled and cut
  into tiny dice
2 tablespoons finely chopped well-drained
  sun-dried tomatoes packed in oil
2 teaspoons shredded fresh coriander
squeeze of lemon juice
salt and freshly ground black pepper

To finish

extra virgin olive oil
coarse sea salt

First prepare the clam vinaigrette. Wash the clams, then put them in a pan, cover and cook until the shells open. Remove the meat from the shells and set aside. Reserve the clam liquor from the shells.

Heat 1 tablespoon olive oil in a small pan and soften the onion and garlic without colouring. Tip into a bowl. Add the potato and stir to mix, then add the tomatoes, clams and coriander. Moisten with 2 tablespoons of the clam liquor and a little more olive oil. Season with lemon juice, salt and pepper. Set aside.

Preheat the oven to 240°C/gas mark 9.

Make sure the sea bass fillets are dry, then spread softened butter over the skin side. Generously season both sides. Take a frying pan with an ovenproof handle, large enough to hold all 4 fillets comfortably, and heat a generous film of oil for shallow frying. When the oil is hot (but not smoking), put in the fillets, buttered side down. Turn down the heat and cook until the skin crisps nicely, then turn the fillets over on to the flesh side to sear for 1½ minutes. Turn the fillets back over on to the skin side again. Transfer the pan to the oven to cook for 2½ minutes. (If you prefer, you can finish the cooking on top of the stove, but take care not to overcook.)

While you are cooking the fish, put the asparagus spears into a pan of boiling salted water and blanch for about 4 minutes or until just tender (cooking time will depend on the thickness of the spears). Drain and refresh quickly in cold water. Keep hot.

To serve, place 4 asparagus spears down one side of each plate and a line of clam vinaigrette down the other side. Lay a fish fillet on top, on a diagonal across the two. Sprinkle the fish and asparagus with good extra virgin olive oil and coarse sea salt.

A stiff fish, firm to the feel, is a fresh fish. To test, hold it up by the tail; it should stand straight. In my kitchen, if a fish isn't fresh, it goes straight back to the fishmonger. I only use line-caught sea bass which have come into shore to feed – when trawlered, the fish bellies are full and this could taint the flesh of the fish before the boat reaches harbour and the fish is sold. In the restaurant we finish this dish with a ring of tomato oil, made by blending our own oven-dried tomatoes with olive oil.

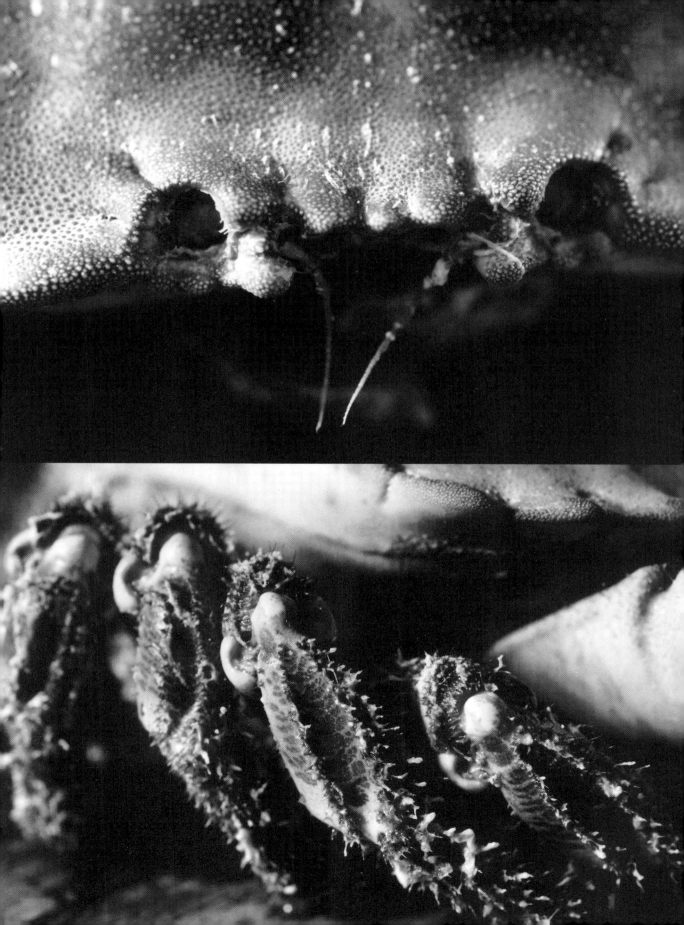

John Dory with crab juices

Serves 4

1 Cornish crab (about 700 g), cooked

unsalted butter

mirepoix of 1 tablespoon each finely

chopped shallot, mushrooms,

fennel and celery

5 tomatoes, 4 of them chopped and

1 peeled, seeded and neatly diced

1 tablespoon brandy

about 300 ml light fish stock or water

sunflower oil

2 medium John Dory (about 1.3 kg),

filleted

$^1/_2$ teaspoon chopped fresh chives

$^1/_4$ teaspoon chopped fresh tarragon

$^1/_4$ teaspoon chopped fresh dill

salt and freshly ground black pepper

John Dory is getting to be very expensive, and as it has a high bone content (about three-quarters of the total weight is unusable bone) you must be choosy in selecting your fish. Turbot can be used instead, if you want to be sure of a good bit of meaty fish.

Crack open the crab shell and remove all the meat. Pick it over to be sure there are no bits of shell or cartilage, then set aside. Using the back, blunt edge of a large, heavy knife, coarsely crush the crab shell.

Melt a knob of butter in a large saucepan, add the mirepoix and cook over a low heat for about 10 minutes or until softened and lightly coloured. Add the crushed crab shells and chopped tomatoes, and cook for 1-2 minutes, stirring. Add the brandy, warm it briefly and then set alight. Pour in enough stock or water to cover the ingredients. Bring to the boil and simmer for 20 minutes.

Strain through a fine sieve into a clean pan. Bring back to the boil and boil to reduce by half. Whisk in another knob of butter. Season and keep warm.

Heat a film of sunflower oil in a heavy-based frying pan. Sauté the fish fillets for 3 minutes on each side. Add the crab meat and cook for a further 2 minutes to heat it through, stirring.

To serve, arrange the fish fillets and crab meat on hot plates. Add the diced tomatoes and herbs to the sauce, stir and pour over the fish.

Dover sole roasted on the bone with brown shrimps and cucumber

Serves 4

1 cucumber

pinch of sugar

unsalted butter

4 Dover soles, 350-400 g each,
   skinned on both sides, trimmed
   and head removed

dry white wine

225 g brown shrimps, cooked
   and peeled

1 tablespoon chopped fresh dill

For the butter sauce

3 shallots, peeled and very
   finely chopped

3 black peppercorns, finely crushed

100 ml dry white wine

120 g unsalted butter, chilled

squeeze of lemon juice

pinch of cayenne pepper

salt and freshly ground black pepper

Peel the cucumber, then cut it in half lengthways and scoop out the seeds with the tip of a teaspoon. Cut into tiny balls and blanch briefly in boiling water. Alternatively, shred into 'spaghetti' using a mandoline. Put in a colander, sprinkle with the sugar and a little salt, and toss with your fingers. Leave to drain for 10-15 minutes. The cucumber will go limp.

Preheat the oven to 180°C/gas mark 4.

Take an earthenware dish large enough to hold the soles in one layer, and butter it lightly. Put in the fish, seasoned on both sides, and sprinkle with a little white wine. Cover with greaseproof paper and roast for 15-20 minutes.

Cooking fish like Dover sole and plaice on the bone gives a really good flavour and retains the succulence – it seems very natural just to put it on a dish and bake it. The cucumber and brown shrimps with the fish are a perfect marriage. If we have any girolles, we toss them in a bit of butter until they exude juice, then add them too.

Meanwhile, to make the sauce, combine the shallots, peppercorns and wine in a saucepan, and boil until the wine has evaporated. Holding the butter in one hand and a whisk in the other, squeeze the butter through your fingers into the pan, whisking it into the shallots. When all the butter has been added, season with the lemon juice, cayenne and salt. If the sauce shows signs of splitting, whisk in a sprinkling of hot water. Remove from the heat. Add the shrimps and dill to the sauce and stir to mix. Keep the sauce warm, covered with cling film.

Warm through the balls of cucumber, or spaghetti, with just a touch of butter, tossing gently. Season.

To serve, put the sole on hot plates and spoon the cucumber on top. Add 1 tablespoon of the sole cooking juices to the sauce and spoon over all. Serve with boiled new potatoes.

Sautéed veal kidney with shallot cream and chorizo

1 veal kidney in its fat
50 g good farmhouse chorizo,
skinned and sliced into
rounds, then into strips
2 tablespoons extra virgin olive oil
1/2 head Savoy cabbage, finely shredded
sunflower oil
chopped fresh tarragon to garnish

Serves 4

For the shallot cream
unsalted butter
280 g shallots, peeled and chopped
1 garlic clove, peeled and chopped
6 tablespoons whipping cream
1 teaspoon chopped fresh tarragon
salt and freshly ground black pepper

Be sure to buy the kidney still in its wrapping of creamy fat, as this guarantees it is fresh. Our chorizo is made by an artisan producer in the Pyrenees. What you can buy in the supermarket is a very poor relation, so if possible, get it from a good importer of Spanish foods.

Remove the fat from the kidney, together with all the gristle and core. Separate the lobes of the kidney, in their original shape, keeping them about the same size, if possible. Take off the thin outer membrane. Cover and keep in the fridge until ready to cook.

Moisten the strips of chorizo in the olive oil, then set aside to macerate while you make the shallot cream.

Melt a knob of butter in a heavy-based saucepan and sweat the shallots and garlic over a low heat until very soft but not coloured. Add the whipping cream and stir to moisten. Add the tarragon and season with salt and pepper. Purée in a food processor, then return to the pan and keep warm.

Blanch the cabbage in boiling water for 1 minute, then drain well and refresh in cold water. Set aside.

Season the prepared kidneys with salt and pepper. Heat a film of sunflower oil in a heavy-based frying pan and sauté the kidneys over a high heat for about 3 minutes, stirring and tossing to sear and brown all sides. Remove from the heat and leave to rest at the side of the cooker for 3 minutes.

Meanwhile, drain the oil from the chorizo into a pan, heat and add the cabbage. Toss to warm through, then add the chorizo and toss together. Reheat the shallot cream, if necessary.

To serve, drizzle some of the shallot cream round the edge of hot plates (serve the rest separately). Pile the cabbage and chorizo in the middle. Cut the kidneys in half and place on the cabbage. Finish with a sprinkling of chopped tarragon.

Stephen Bull's rump steak burger with bacon brioche

Serves 4

700 g well-trimmed rump steak

120 g beef bone marrow

unsalted butter

1 small onion, peeled and
   finely chopped

2 teaspoons fresh marjoram leaves

sunflower oil

salt and freshly ground black pepper

To serve

4 slices of Bacon Brioche
   (see page 200), toasted

Troisgros Courgette Chutney
   (see page 37)

Preheat the oven to 230°C/gas mark 8.

Be sure the steak is trimmed of all sinew and fat. Using a large sharp knife, chop the meat until it has a very fine minced texture. Place in a bowl. Grate the bone marrow directly into the bowl.

Heat a small knob of butter in a small pan and sweat the onion with the marjoram until soft but not coloured. Cool slightly, then add to the meat in the bowl. Season well. Mix together with your hands, without squeezing, then divide into four and shape each portion lightly into a thick patty like a tournedos, about 2.5 cm thick. Do not press together or the steak burgers will be tough.

Heat a film of oil in a frying pan with an ovenproof handle. Sear and brown the burgers gently on both sides, then transfer the pan to the oven and finish cooking – 3 minutes for rare and 5 minutes for medium rare.

Set each steak burger on a slice of toasted brioche and serve with the chutney.

This is one of the first dishes we had on the menu in Stephen Bull's restaurant in Blandford Street, London. It took a lot of reworking to get it right. Beef marrow adds moisture and flavour to the burgers. They must not be overcooked – if cooked well done, the marrow will ooze out of the meat. The sharp chutney is a good partner for the rich burger.

Young turnips with amontillado

Serves 4

20-24 navets (small young turnips)
unsalted butter
1 tablespoon sugar
1 $^{1}/_{2}$ tablespoons amontillado sherry
salt and freshly ground black pepper

When adding alcohol to a dish, I like to put it in at the end, so that the taste of the alcohol stays fresh and you can control the final flavour. It's like adding layers. This simple veg dish is brilliant with warm shellfish.

Trim the ends of the turnips, leaving a little of the green. Wash the turnips, scraping or rubbing them with a green scouring pad to remove just the top layer of skin.

Put the turnips in a saucepan and pour over boiling salted water to three-quarters cover them. Add 2 generous knobs of butter, the sugar and salt and pepper to taste. Bring back to the boil, then reduce the heat and simmer for 5 minutes.

Add the sherry and tilt the pan to mix the sherry into the cooking liquid. Simmer for a further 1-2 minutes.

Lift out the turnips with a draining spoon, and serve hot with a little of the cooking liquid spooned over.

Green pea and marjoram purée

Serves 4

400 g podded fresh peas (about 900 g
   in pods)
15 g fresh marjoram
chicken or vegetable stock or water
2 tablespoons double cream (optional)
salt and freshly ground black pepper

Cook the peas in boiling salted water for 5-8 minutes or until tender (cooking time will depend on the size and age of the peas). Drain and refresh. Put the peas in a blender or food processor with the leaves picked from the marjoram. Blend to a purée. If the mixture is too thick to blend easily, add a few drops of stock or water. Season to taste with salt and pepper, then put back into the saucepan (or a microwave bowl).

You can leave out the cream here – it is only to enrich, not to let down, or thin, the purée. The best way to reheat this is in a microwave.

Stir in the cream to enrich, if using, and reheat gently for serving.

Salad of greens and herbs

salad leaves such as baby spinach leaves,
Cos/Romaine, ice lettuce,
watercress, wild rocket and mizuna
(but definitely not Lollo Rosso,
iceberg, radicchio or chicory)
finely chopped shallots
snipped fresh chives

fresh chervil leaves
coarsely chopped fresh flat-leaf parsley
For the dressing
3 parts best olive oil
1 part lemon juice
a touch of sugar
salt and freshly ground black pepper

It's impossible to talk about amounts here – you must decide these for yourself. Just be sure to use salad leaves and herbs that are as fresh as they can possibly be, and ideally those grown with little or no chemical treatment.

Combine the salad leaves, shallots and herbs in a big salad bowl. Add salt and pepper to taste, and toss the greens to be sure the seasoning is dispersed properly.

Make the dressing by whisking the oil, lemon juice and sugar together in a small bowl.

Add the dressing to the salad, toss and serve.

White peaches with raspberries and Champagne sorbet

Serves 8

4 ripe but firm white peaches

1 bottle (75 cl) Champagne or
   good sparkling wine

500 g caster sugar

1 vanilla pod, split open

400 g raspberries

lemon juice if needed

400 ml double cream

icing sugar to taste

Put the peaches in a bowl. Pour over boiling water to cover and leave for about 20 seconds, then drain and put into a bowl of iced water. Gently peel off the skins; reserve the skins.

White peaches are a little less sweet than yellow ones, but they have a delicious perfume. Make this on the day you are going to serve it.

Put the Champagne and sugar in a saucepan and add the peach skins. Scrape the tiny seeds out of the vanilla pod into the pan, then add the pod too. Bring just to the boil, stirring to dissolve the sugar. Add the peaches and poach at a very gentle bubble for about 5 minutes or until just tender – a cocktail stick should go through easily. Turn them over in the syrup occasionally as they poach. Remove from the heat and leave to cool in the syrup.

Meanwhile, put 250 g of the raspberries in a food processor with 2-3 tablespoons of the poaching syrup and blend to a purée. Press the purée through a fine nylon sieve. Taste and add more poaching syrup and a squeeze of lemon juice, if necessary. Set the raspberry sauce aside.

Lift the peaches out of the syrup with a slotted spoon. Cut them in half and remove the stones. Cover and set aside at room temperature.

Strain the poaching liquid through a fine sieve, then chill it. When it is cold, taste it. It should have a good Champagne flavour, so add a little more if needed. Add a squeeze of lemon juice too if it seems too sweet. The liquid should be strongly flavoured as freezing will diminish it. Pour into an ice-cream machine and freeze. Once softly frozen, transfer to a freezerproof container and put into the freezer to 'mature' for an hour or so. If freezing for longer than 1 hour, transfer the sorbet to the fridge 20 minutes before serving to soften slightly.

Meanwhile, put the remaining raspberries in a bowl with the cream and sweeten with about 1 tablespoon icing sugar, or to taste. Whip together until the cream is thick and streaked with raspberry juice; the texture should not be smooth.

To serve, spoon the raspberry 'fool' into soup plates or dessert glasses and top each with a peach half and a scoop of sorbet. Drizzle the raspberry sauce over the peaches.

Vanilla cream pots with blackcurrant compote

Serves 4-6

500 ml double cream

100 ml milk

½ vanilla pod, split open

6 egg yolks

75 g caster sugar

For the blackcurrant compote

150 g blackcurrants removed
   from their stalks

crème de cassis

sugar to taste

Pour the cream and milk into a heavy-based saucepan. Scrape the tiny seeds out of the vanilla pod into the cream, then add the pod too. Heat until bubbles start to form round the edge of the pan, then remove from the heat and set aside to infuse for 20 minutes.

Meanwhile, whisk the egg yolks with the sugar until thick and a pale lemon colour.

Preheat the oven to 170°C/gas mark 3.

Remove the vanilla pod from the hot cream mixture, then pour into the yolks, stirring to mix. Strain the custard, then ladle into deep mousse pots with lids or ramekins, each about 150 ml capacity. Cover the pots with the lids, or seal each ramekin with foil, to prevent a skin from forming. Set in a roasting tin (bain marie) containing enough hot water to come half way up the sides of the pots. Bake for 40-60 minutes or until set but still 'quivery' when shaken. Remove from the bain marie, then leave to cool before chilling for at least 2 hours.

Meanwhile, prepare the compote. Put half of the blackcurrants in a bowl and sprinkle with crème de cassis. Leave to macerate for 2 hours.

Put the remaining blackcurrants in a saucepan with sugar to taste. Bring to the boil, stirring to dissolve the sugar. Remove from the heat and sieve. Allow to cool.

Add the blackcurrant purée to the cassis-soaked blackcurrants and check for sweetness. Chill until about 30 minutes before serving.

To serve, spoon the compote on top of the vanilla cream pots.

The blackcurrant compote should be a tart-sweet contrast to the rich cream pots, so when making the purée add just a little sugar as you can sweeten it more later.

Cherries in Riesling with goat's cheese ice-cream

Serves 6-8

1 kg ripe but firm, sweet cherries

1 bottle (75 cl) Riesling

100 g caster sugar

1 vanilla pod, split in half

1 tablespoon grenadine

7 teaspoons arrowroot mixed
with 4 teaspoons water

Wholemeal tuiles (see page 205)
or Brittany sablés
(see page 205) for serving

For the ice-cream

200 g sugar

300 g ripe, strong-flavoured goat's
cheese (weight without rind)

fresh lime juice if needed

Use a goat's cheese that has a soft, oozy texture, not one that is dry and crumbly. Make the ice-cream on the day of serving.

Stone the cherries, keeping them as whole as possible. Set the cherries aside in a bowl. Put the stones in a heavy polythene bag and set them on a wooden board. Hit with the base of a heavy pot to crush them coarsely. Pour the crushed stones into a saucepan and add the wine, sugar, vanilla pod and grenadine. Bring to the boil, stirring to dissolve the sugar. Remove from the heat, add the arrowroot mixture and bring back to the boil, stirring until thickened. Strain the syrup over the cherries through a fine sieve. Cover and set aside in the fridge to macerate for 2-3 hours.

Meanwhile, make the ice-cream. Put the sugar and 200 ml water in a pan and bring to the boil, stirring to dissolve the sugar. Remove from the heat and leave to cool completely. Put the goat's cheese in a bowl and mash it, then whisk in three-quarters of the cold sugar syrup until smooth. Continue adding the rest of the syrup gradually, tasting the mixture as you go – it should have a good flavour of goat's cheese and be just sweet enough. A little lime juice may be needed to add a touch of sharpness. Press through a sieve. Pour into an ice-cream machine and freeze. Once softly frozen, transfer to a freezerproof container and put into the freezer to 'mature' for an hour or so. If freezing for longer than 1 hour, transfer the ice-cream to the fridge 20 minutes before serving to soften slightly.

To serve, ladle the cherries and syrup into soup plates and add a quenelle or scoop of ice-cream to the centre of each. Serve with tuiles or sablés.

Almond macaroons with mascarpone mousse and strawberries

For the macaroons
100 g ground almonds
1 heaped teaspoon cornflour
2 egg whites
squeeze of lemon juice
pinch of salt
200 g caster sugar
For the mousse
150 g full-fat soft cheese (Philadelphia)
150 g mascarpone

75 ml thick Crème anglaise, made with
half milk and half double cream
(see page 202)
40 g caster sugar
To serve
400 g fresh, ripe strawberries
1-2 tablespoons icing sugar
squeeze of lemon juice
chopped unsalted pistachio nuts
cocoa powder

This is a delicious dessert. It looks impressive, but is really quite easy to make. My children love these macaroons.

To make the macaroons, sift the ground almonds with the cornflour. Set aside. Whisk the egg whites with the lemon juice and salt until frothy, then gradually whisk in one-third of the sugar and continue whisking until the meringue will hold a soft peak. Add another third of the sugar and whisk until the meringue is thick and glossy. Add the remaining sugar and whisk to a stiff peak. Fold in the sifted ground almonds.

Put the almond meringue into a piping bag fitted with an 8 mm plain nozzle. Set a siliconised or other non-stick liner on a large baking sheet, or line it with greased greaseproof paper. Pipe the meringue on to the baking sheet in 5 cm diameter rounds, to make 16 macaroons. Let stand for 20 minutes so that the macaroons can dry slightly and form a bit of a crust.

Preheat the oven to 190°C/gas mark 5.

Place the macaroons in the oven and turn the heat down to 130°C/gas mark 1. Bake for 15-20 minutes or until just off-white and slightly dry to the touch, but not as dry as meringues. Set aside to cool.

For the mousse, whisk together all the ingredients until evenly blended. Keep in the fridge until ready to serve.

Hull the strawberries. Reserve 100 g of them for the decoration, and purée the remainder in a food processor. Add icing sugar to taste and a squeeze of lemon juice, then blend again briefly. Press the purée through a fine nylon sieve.

To serve, sandwich together pairs of almond macaroons with the mousse. Set a macaroon 'sandwich' in the centre of each plate and dust with cocoa powder. Slice the reserved strawberries and arrange round the macaroons. Dress the strawberries with the strawberry sauce and finish with a sprinkling of pistachios.

Sorbet of charentais melon

Serves 6

2 large ripe charentais melons
   (about 700 g each)
juice of 1 lemon
180 g caster sugar
For the strawberry sauce
300 g ripe strawberries
icing sugar
lemon juice

Peel the melons, cut them in half and remove the seeds from the centre. Weigh out 500 g of melon flesh (keep the rest for serving). Put the melon flesh, lemon juice and sugar in a food processor and blend to a purée. Press the purée through a fine sieve. Pour into an ice-cream machine and freeze. Once softly frozen, transfer to a freezerproof container and put into the freezer to 'mature' for an hour or so. If freezing for longer than 1 hour, transfer the sorbet to the fridge 20 minutes before serving to soften slightly.

This simple sorbet has a rich colour and pure melon flavour. You must use a perfectly ripe, beautifully perfumed charentais. Make the sorbet on the day you are going to serve it.

While the sorbet is freezing, hull the strawberries and put them in the food processor. Blend to a purée. Add icing sugar to taste and a squeeze of lemon juice, then blend again briefly. Press the purée through a fine nylon sieve.

To serve, shape quenelles, or take scoops, of the sorbet and arrange on plates with slices of melon. Drizzle round the strawberry sauce.

Summer wine

The pleasure of wine with food lies in serendipitously discovering a marriage that works for you. You can have a bacon butty with a great burgundy and find a match made in heaven. However, we should try to seek out wines that have a distinctive cultural heritage, wherein the individuality of the grower is expressed, where substance precedes commerce and also where sustainable and preferably organic methods of viticulture are being employed – in short, wines in touch with their roots. Promoting a living food and wine culture is all about recognising, understanding and choosing quality, and appreciating the rhythm of the seasons themselves.

Summer is a tricky time for wine selection. Since hefty alcoholic reds and whites are often volatile during warmer or unsettled weather, less complex, fruitier and more refreshing wines become attractive to drink. Nevertheless, although we may prefer instant gratification instead of demanding subtlety, the profusion of top-notch fresh ingredients on our menus, such as lobster, crab, Dover sole, sea bass, young peas, baby broad beans and fresh herbs, calls for fairly robust wines with decent concentration and structure. Pick a good white Burgundy with a touch of buttery oak: Saint-Aubin, for example, or a village Puligny or a Pouilly-Fuissé from one of the best producers. The combination of beautifully fresh fish and white Burgundy is an elegant, natural marriage, the sweet texture of the flesh meshing with the mineral complexity and smokiness of the wine.

If the sun is shining and you are outdoors on a terrace or in the garden, quenching thirst is the main aim. A good perky rosé will capture the light and lift the spirits. This is also, of course, a good time of year to savour light wines with a refreshing sweetness: a delicate honey-threaded German Riesling Spätlese or a Vouvray demi-sec from a top grower, as well as some delicious English wines. Up several notches on the alcohol scale, dry Chenin Blanc, particularly Savennieres or Saumur Blanc, is a magnificent accompaniment to wild salmon, whilst Jurançon is most appealing with freshwater fish like trout and pike.

If your inclination is to serve a buttery terrine or kidneys with a red, a more-ish Dolcetto or a garrigue-scented Provence wine might suffice, but I would prefer an earthy sweet-sour Barbera d'Alba or a piny red Bandol from Provence.

Douglas Wregg

Summer cheese

Ireland is the home to some of the finest cheeses. There seems to be something special in the land and the climate, most particularly in west Cork. Excellent cheeses are made in this extreme western tip of Europe, many of them soft cheeses, with a 'washed rind' – the pungent, pinkish-orange surface also found on French cheeses such as Livarot.

West Cork has attracted a lively and diverse collection of people, the type of people who are more likely to take up the strange craft of cheesemaking. Not only is it a beautiful county, but the land produces the good milk that makes good cheese. On top of that the atmosphere is cool but not cold and damp – ideal conditions for maturing cheeses.

Three cheeses in particular typify the area, each made on one of the fingers of land you see on the bottom left-hand corner of a map of Ireland. The cheesemaking began on the Beara peninsula with Norman and Veronica Steele, on their small farm on the side of a mountain called Mishkish. Veronica was trying to make a hard cheese, but a pinkish rind kept growing on it, encouraged by the wet climate. In the end she gave in to it and now makes the superb and complex pinkish-orange cheese called Milleens.

Other similar but distinct cheeses followed. Durrus, made by Jeffa Bates on the Sheeps Head peninsula south of the Beara, is fatter and thicker than Milleens, with a thicker, leathery crust. It has a delicious rich, sweet flavour. South again to the Mizen peninsula and you find Gubbeen, made by Tom and Giana Ferguson on their farm near Schull. Firmer than the other cheeses, with a pinker rind, Gubbeen has a lovely smell of mushrooms and a milky sweet flavour.

Summer is a difficult time for many cheeses and quality varies hugely with how wet or dry, how hot or cold the summer is. Generally, though, the soft goat's milk cheeses made in summer are wonderful.

Tymsboro
Perroche
Golden Cross
Ragstone

Randolph Hodgson, Neal's Yard Dairy

the fat flocks   and the fields' fatness

autumn

best in autumn

plaice **skate** herring **eel** sprats **native oysters** mussels **scallops** hare **rabbit** venison **wild duck** grouse **partridge** pigeon **quail** snipe **pheasant** cauliflower **broccoli** carrots **parsnips** turnips **Brussels sprouts** pumpkins courgettes **tomatoes** plums **damsons** greengages **apples** dessert pears **grapes** hazelnuts

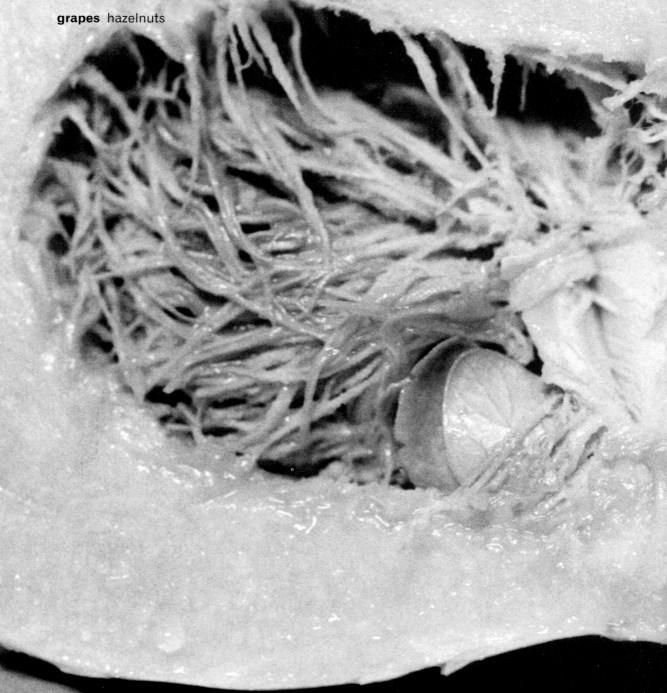

Oysters with sauerkraut and red wine

Serves 4

20 native oysters (number 2)

2 thin slices cooking pancetta, cut into very fine strips

Pickled white cabbage (see page 204)

For the red wine butter sauce

2 shallots, peeled and finely chopped

pinch of fresh thyme leaves

$^{1}/_{2}$ garlic clove, peeled and finely chopped

100 ml red wine (medium-bodied Pinot Noir-type)

120 g unsalted butter, chilled

pinch of sugar

salt and freshly ground black pepper

Very rarely do I ever think of serving native oysters hot, but this is one exception. This needs the subtlety and clarity of natives; Pacific oysters will not do.

Using an oyster knife, open the oysters and tip them into a bowl with all the liquor from their shells. Cover the bowl and keep the oysters in the fridge until ready to cook. Scrub the bottom shells and reserve.

Cook the strips of pancetta in a hot dry pan until they are crisp. Drain on kitchen paper and set aside.

For the sauce, put the shallots, garlic, thyme and wine in a small saucepan and boil until the wine has almost completely evaporated. Reduce the heat to very low. Holding the butter in one hand and a whisk in the other, squeeze the butter through your fingers into the pan, whisking it into the shallots. When all the butter has been added, season with the sugar, salt and pepper. If the sauce shows signs of splitting, whisk in a sprinkling of hot water. Remove from the heat and keep warm.

Reheat the pickled cabbage. Tip the oysters and their liquor into another pan and warm for about 30 seconds, just until the edges start to curl. Drain the oysters and stir the liquor into the cabbage.

To serve, drain the cabbage and put a spoonful into each oyster shell. Set an oyster on top and spoon over the sauce. Finish with the crisp strips of pancetta.

Polenta with braised hare

Serves 6

For the braised hare
1 hare
sunflower oil
mirepoix of 100 g each onion, celery
   and carrot, cut into large dice
plain flour
175 ml red wine (Cabernet
   Sauvignon-type)
brown stock

1 fresh bouquet garni of thyme,
   parsley and bay leaf
For the polenta
2 garlic cloves, peeled and crushed
1/2 teaspoon fresh thyme leaves
250 g polenta (not instant)
25-40 g Parmesan, freshly grated
80 g mascarpone
salt and freshly ground black pepper

Have your butcher joint the hare for you, halving the legs at the thigh, leaving the front whole and cutting the saddle into 4 pieces. Trim off the belly flaps.

Preheat the oven to 170°C/gas mark 3.

Season the pieces of hare with salt and pepper. Heat a film of sunflower oil in a heavy-based flameproof casserole. Put in the hare pieces and brown slowly on all sides. Remove to a colander to drain.

Add the mirepoix to the casserole and cook until softened and browned. Return the hare pieces to the pot. Dust lightly with flour and cook for 2-3 minutes, stirring and turning the hare and vegetables. Pour in the wine, bring to the boil and reduce until almost completely evaporated. Add enough brown stock to cover the hare pieces and put in the bouquet garni. Bring back to the boil, skimming off any impurities. Cover the casserole with greaseproof paper and then the lid. Transfer to the oven to braise for 1½ hours.

Remove the hare pieces from the casserole and cool slightly, then pick the meat off the bones, keeping the pieces as large as possible. Put the meat in a heavy-based pan. Strain in just enough of the cooking liquid to cover. (The left-over liquid is heaven – use it as a game stock for a lentil and hare soup or another game dish.) Set aside.

To cook the polenta, bring 1.5 litres of water to the boil in a large saucepan. Add the garlic, thyme and 1 teaspoon salt. Stirring the water constantly with a whisk, gradually rain in the polenta. When all has been added, reduce the heat to very low and cook gently for 20-30 minutes, stirring frequently with a wooden spoon. The polenta is ready when it comes away from the side of the pan.

About 10 minutes before the polenta has finished cooking, reheat the braised hare and check the seasoning.

As an Irishman, I generally prefer potatoes with everything, but I do use polenta a bit. It works well here, although you could also serve the braised hare with colcannon (see the recipe on page 182). This could be served as a main course for 4.

Add the Parmesan and mascarpone to the polenta and stir until smooth. Ladle the braised hare into deep soup plates and spoon the polenta on top.

For cornmeal cakes, make the polenta as above, using 750 ml water, 125 g polenta and 15-25 g Parmesan; leave out the mascarpone. Pour into an oiled shallow tray to make a layer about 1 cm thick. Cover with cling film and press to spread out evenly – if your tin is very shallow, with just a little raised edge, you can roll over the polenta with a rolling pin. Chill until set firm. Using a 5 cm pastry cutter, stamp out rounds (or other shapes if you prefer). Dust lightly with flour, then fry very gently in a lightly oiled non-stick pan until golden brown and crisp on both sides. I serve these with the Saddle of rabbit stuffed with black pudding on page 170.

Hot duck foie gras with apple, lime and shredded sorrel

Serves 4

5 tablespoons white wine (Sauvignon Blanc)	2 tablespoons cornflour, mixed with $1\frac{1}{2}$ tablespoons water
5 tablespoons apple juice	2 Granny Smith apples, peeled, cored and thinly sliced
juice of 3 limes	
6 tablespoons sugar	400 g piece of foie gras, well chilled
small knob of unsalted butter	75 g fresh sorrel, finely shredded

Combine the wine, apple juice, lime juice, sugar and butter in a wide pan and heat gently, stirring to dissolve the sugar. Add the cornflour and bring to the boil, stirring until thickened. Add the sliced apples and leave to cook over a low heat for 4 minutes or until slightly softened. Set aside.

Heat a well-seasoned cast-iron griddle or other heavy pan (not non-stick) for 5-10 minutes or until smoking hot. Meanwhile, take the foie gras from the fridge. It should be hard, like chilled butter. Cut it into four equal slices. Slap the pieces of foie gras on the hot griddle. They will smoke a lot, so be sure the extractor fan is on full! Once on the griddle don't move the foie gras about. After about 30 seconds, gently lift the edge of one of the pieces to check the underside. If it is a rich golden brown, turn the pieces over to colour the other side. This may take a little bit longer than the first side. The foie gras is cooked when it just gives to the touch. If it still feels a bit hard in the centre, remove the pan from the heat and leave the foie gras to one side for another 30 seconds or so to finish cooking.

Lift the apple slices out of the syrup and arrange on plates in a fan shape. Top with the foie gras. Spoon a little syrup over the apples. Surround with a ring of sorrel and serve immediately.

The tart syrup here is a beautiful contrast with the rich foie gras. Use the fat from the foie gras left in the griddle to make a confit or when roasting potatoes.

Pumpkin gnocchi with langoustines

Serves 4

For the gnocchi

1 pumpkin (500-750 g), seeds
  and fibres removed
275 g floury potatoes, cut in
  half if large
1 egg yolk
25 g Parmesan, freshly grated
25 g plain flour

For the langoustines

sunflower oil

12-20 fresh raw langoustines
  (3-5 each)
mirepoix of 4 tablespoons each finely
  chopped onion, celery and fennel
1 garlic clove, peeled and crushed
1 tablespoon tomato purée
1 tablespoon brandy
4 tablespoons double cream
1 sprig of fresh tarragon
salt and freshly ground black pepper

Preheat the oven to 180°C/gas mark 4.

Cut the pumpkin into large pieces and wrap in foil. Bake until soft and tender, about 1½ hours. Unwrap and leave until cool enough to handle, then scrape all the flesh from the skin; discard the skin. Press the pumpkin flesh through a sieve into a muslin-lined bowl (or purée in a mouli-légumes). Tie the muslin into a bag and leave the pumpkin purée to drip overnight, set over the bowl to catch the juices.

The next day, put the unpeeled potatoes into a pan of salted water, bring to the boil and simmer for 20-25 minutes or until tender. Drain and return to the empty pan, off the heat. Cover with a tea towel (or newspaper) and leave to steam and dry off for 5 minutes. Then uncover and leave until cool enough to handle. Peel the potatoes and put them through a mouli-légumes or potato ricer into a bowl. You should have about 250 g potato.

Weigh the drained pumpkin purée; you want about 250 g (reserve the juice). Add to the potato, together with the egg yolk, Parmesan, flour and a seasoning of salt and

pepper. Mix well together. Flour your hands, then roll the pumpkin mixture into balls about 2.5 cm in diameter. Bring a large pan of salted water to the boil and add a few drops of oil. Add the gnocchi to the water and cook for about 2-4 minutes or until they rise to the surface. Drain, plunge briefly into ice-cold water to stop the cooking and then drain again. Dry on kitchen paper. Set aside, covered loosely with cling film, while you make the sauce.

Pull the heads off the langoustines (keep the heads), then drop into a pan of boiling salted water and cook for 2 minutes. Drain and refresh. The langoustines will be

Use a small pumpkin or a piece from a medium-size pumpkin for the gnocchi – the very large, Hallowe'en pumpkins can be very fibrous. The gnocchi should be cooked very soon after shaping, or they will fall apart. If more convenient, the sauce can be made first.

undercooked, but firm. Peel the langoustines (keep all the shells), then cover and set aside. Put the langoustine heads and shells in a food processor and chop coarsely.

Heat a film of oil in a saucepan, add the mirepoix and garlic, and soften without colouring. Add the chopped langoustine shells and the tomato purée, and stir round to mix with the vegetables and oil. Add the brandy, warm it briefly and set alight. Leave to burn until the flame is extinguished. Measure the juices drained from the pumpkin and make up to 250 ml with water. Add to the pan, then enrich with the cream and stir to mix. Add the tarragon. Heat until bubbles start to form round the edge of the pan, then remove from the heat and leave to infuse for 30 minutes, stirring now and then.

Strain the sauce through a fine sieve into a clean pan. Check the seasoning. Reheat the sauce to just below boiling point, then add the gnocchi and heat for 3 minutes. Drop in the langoustines and warm through for 30 seconds. Serve in soup plates.

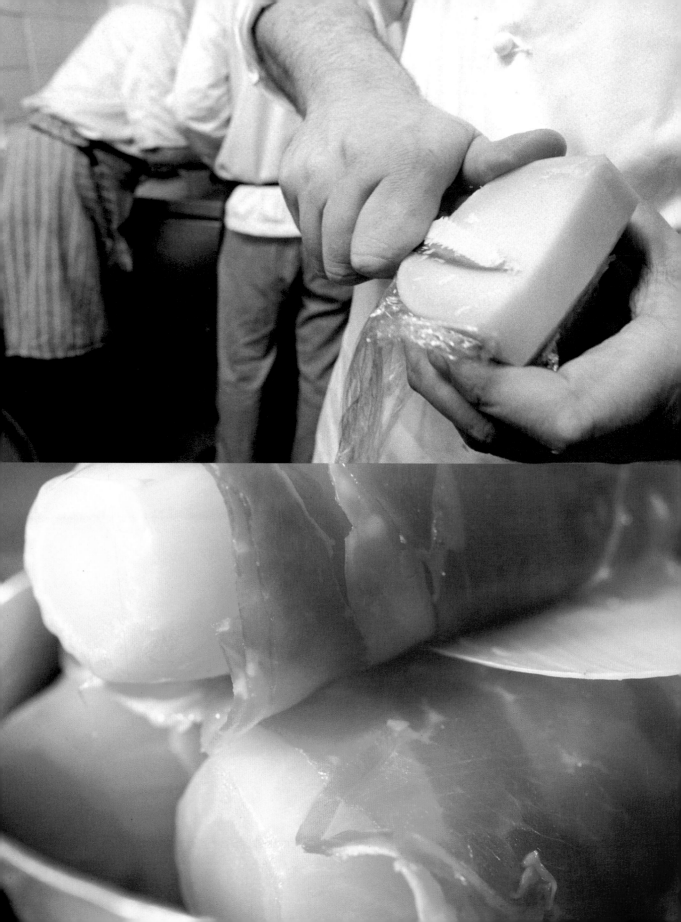

Chicory wrapped in baked English ham

Serves 4

8 small heads of chicory, bases
trimmed and outer leaves removed
8 thin slices baked English ham
170 g Irish Gruyère-type cheese
For the béchamel
500 ml milk
slice of onion

1 bay leaf
a few sprigs of fresh thyme
40 g unsalted butter
40 g plain flour
freshly grated nutmeg
cayenne pepper
salt and freshly ground black pepper

This is a simple dish – comfort food of the highest order. It is a hearty starter, and would make a great supper dish too. There is an Irish version of Gruyère, called Gabriel, that I would use here. If you cannot find it, use Gruyère.

To make the béchamel, put the milk, onion, bay leaf and thyme in a heavy-based saucepan and heat until bubbles form round the edge. Remove from the heat, cover the pan and set aside to infuse for 20 minutes.

Meanwhile, blanch the chicory in boiling salted water for 4 minutes. Drain and refresh, then squeeze each head gently to remove excess water. Season the chicory, then wrap each head in a slice of ham. Arrange in one layer in a buttered baking dish, packing the heads in tightly.

Preheat the oven to 180°C/gas mark 4.

Strain the flavoured milk into a jug. Clean the pan, and melt the butter in it. Add the flour and stir well, then cook gently for 2 minutes. Gradually add the hot milk, whisking constantly. Bring to the boil, then reduce the heat and simmer for 4-5 minutes, whisking frequently. Season with salt, pepper, nutmeg and a touch of cayenne. Grate a few tablespoons of the cheese, add to the sauce and stir until melted.

Spoon the sauce over the ham-wrapped chicory, not covering them completely. Sprinkle evenly with the remaining cheese, grated or cut into shavings. Bake for 25-30 minutes or until the sauce is bubbling round the sides and the cheese is melted and golden brown. Serve hot.

Poached smoked haddock with cardamom rice and crispy shallots, curry-spiced cream

Serves 4

4 large shallots, peeled and sliced
  paper thin
sunflower oil
4 pieces of smoked haddock fillet
  (about 150 g each), skinned

For the curry-spiced cream
sunflower oil
40 g bulb fennel, finely diced
40 g small cauliflower florets
1 small celery stick, trimmed and
  finely diced
40 g finely chopped onion

½ garlic clove, peeled and crushed
piece of fresh red chilli, seeded
1½ teaspoons Madras curry powder
500 ml vegetable stock
4 tablespoons double cream
2 tablespoons chopped fresh coriander

For the cardamom rice
200 g Basmati rice, well rinsed
4-6 cardamom pods
2 eggs, hard-boiled and finely chopped
salt and freshly ground black pepper

First make the cream sauce. Heat a film of oil in a saucepan and sauté the vegetables with the garlic and chilli until soft and just lightly coloured. Add the curry powder as the vegetables start to soften and stir well. Moisten with the stock, then bring to the boil. Stir in the cream and simmer for 5-6 minutes. Strain through a fine sieve into a clean pan (little bits of cauliflower will go through the sieve, but that is fine). Set aside in a deep frying pan.

Push the slices of shallot into rings, then shallow fry until golden and crisp. Do not let them get too dark brown or they will be bitter. Drain on kitchen paper and set aside.

Cook the rice in boiling salted water for 10-12 minutes or until it is tender. Meanwhile, gently toast the cardamom pods in a small dry pan until you can smell their spicy aroma. Tip them on to a cutting board and crack open the pods with the side of a large chef's knife. Scrape the tiny black seeds into a mortar and gently crush with the pestle just to break them up. When the rice is ready, drain it well, then fold in the cardamom seeds, hard-boiled eggs and crispy shallots (do this at the last minute so that the shallots remain crisp).

While the rice is cooking, reheat the cream sauce to a gentle simmer and add the pieces of haddock. Poach gently for 5 minutes. Remove the fish with a fish slice and keep warm. If the sauce is a little thin, boil to reduce it. Check the seasoning and stir in the coriander.

To serve, pile the cardamom rice in the centre of hot soup plates, set the fish on top and spoon over the curry cream sauce.

This is a variation of a kedgeree. The cardamom rice is also good with chicken legs, simply poached in a little stock with coconut milk and fresh red chilli.

Monkfish with split peas

Serves 4

4 pieces of monkfish tail on the bone,
each about 13 cm long,
grey membrane removed

For the vinaigrette

4 tablespoons vegetable oil

1 ½ tablespoons white wine vinegar,
or to taste

¼ teaspoon Dijon mustard

salt and freshly ground black pepper

50 g shallots, peeled and
very finely chopped

3 tablespoons fresh parsley,
finely chopped

For the split peas

200 g dried yellow split peas,
soaked overnight

about 600 ml Ham stock (see page 200)

2 garlic cloves, peeled and chopped

1 carrot, peeled and cut
into 5 mm dice

1 onion, peeled and cut
into 5 mm dice

1 celery stick, trimmed and cut
into 5 mm dice

large knob of unsalted butter

½ teaspoon chopped fresh tarragon

The vinaigrette here is also very good served with hot or cold gammon. If you have any left-over gammon or bacon hock, you can shred the meat and add it to the split peas.

Make the vinaigrette by whisking together the oil, vinegar and mustard. Season to taste, then cover and keep in the fridge until needed. Just before serving, whisk well and add the shallots and parsley.

Preheat the oven to 190°C/gas mark 5. Put a heavy baking tray in to heat.

Drain the soaked split peas and rinse well. Put them in a saucepan with ham stock to cover generously and add the garlic. Bring to the boil, skimming off any scum, then reduce the heat and simmer for 15 minutes. Add the carrot and onion and simmer for a further 10 minutes. Finally, add the celery and simmer for a final 5 minutes. The split peas should have a slightly soupy consistency.

While the split peas are cooking, prepare the monkfish. Season with salt and pepper, then place on the hot baking tray. Cover lightly with greaseproof paper and bake for 8-10 minutes. Remove from the oven and leave to rest for 1-2 minutes.

To finish the split peas, add the butter and tarragon, and tilt the pan to swirl them into the liquid. Check the seasoning. Ladle the split peas into soup plates. Set a monkfish tail on top of each (if you prefer, remove the bone and then cross the pairs of fillets on the split peas). Spoon over the vinaigrette and serve.

Mussel stew with garlic baguette

Serves 4

1 baguette

unsalted butter

1 onion, peeled and very
finely chopped

4 kg fresh mussels, scrubbed and
debearded

125 ml dry white wine

For the parsley and garlic butter

250 g unsalted butter, at room
temperature

50 g fresh parsley, finely chopped

2-4 tsp very finely chopped garlic,
to taste

cayenne pepper

salt and freshly ground pepper

First make the parsley and garlic butter. Beat together the butter, parsley, garlic and a seasoning of cayenne, salt and pepper. Spoon on to a sheet of greaseproof paper and shape into a log, rolling up in the paper. Chill until firm.

Preheat the oven to 180°C/gas mark 4.

Slice the baguette, not cutting all the way through. Reserve about one-quarter of the parsley and garlic butter, and cut the remainder into thin slices. Put a slice of butter in each of the cuts in the baguette. Wrap in foil and bake for 15 minutes.

Meanwhile, melt a knob of butter in a preserving pan or other very large pan, add the onion and sweat until soft. Add the mussels and wine. Cover the pan and cook over a high heat for 3-5 minutes, stirring frequently, until the shells open. Tip the mussels into a colander set over a large bowl to drain. (Discard any mussels whose shells remain stubbornly closed.)

Remove the mussels from their shells and put them into a clean pan. (Add any juices from the shells to the cooking juices in the bowl.) Strain the juices in the bowl through muslin into the pan. Reheat the mussels gently and briefly. At the last minute, add the reserved parsley butter, tilting the pan to swirl it into the sauce. Check the seasoning.

Ladle the mussel stew into soup plates and serve with the garlic baguette.

This is my version of moules marinières – a mussel dish from heaven. Try to use rope-grown mussels, which are fatter than other types and have a fuller flavour. They are also more or less grit-free.

Rib of beef with roasted root vegetables and aged vinegar

Serves 4

1 kg forerib of beef, with 1 rib bone

sunflower oil

small bunch of watercress,
   stalks discarded (optional)

coarse sea salt

For the aged vinegar

120 ml balsamic vinegar

few black peppercorns,
   coarsely crushed

1 garlic clove, peeled

1-2 sprigs of fresh thyme

pinch of sugar

1 teaspoon cornflour mixed with
   1 teaspoon cold water

For the roasted vegetables

duck fat or sunflower oil

2 garlic cloves, peeled

1 small bay leaf

few sprigs of fresh thyme

700 g mixed parsnip, carrot and
   celeriac, peeled and cut into
   5 mm dice

salt and freshly ground black pepper

Preheat the oven to 240°C/gas mark 9.

For the aged vinegar, put the vinegar, peppercorns, garlic, thyme, sugar and a pinch of salt in a small pan and bring to the boil. Remove from the heat and leave to infuse for 5 minutes. Strain the vinegar and return to the pan. Stir in the cornflour mixture, then bring back to the boil, stirring constantly – the vinegar should thicken just enough to coat the back of the spoon. Keep warm.

Season the beef with salt and pepper. Heat a film of oil in a heavy-based frying pan with an ovenproof handle. Put in the beef, and sear and brown on both sides over a high heat. Transfer the pan to the oven and roast for 8-10 minutes (for rare to medium-rare).

Meanwhile, to prepare the vegetables, put enough duck fat into a heavy-based saucepan to cover the vegetables (or put a generous film of oil in the pan). Add the garlic and herbs, and heat the fat. Add the vegetables and cook over a moderate heat, stirring occasionally, until just tender but still firm. Drain and reserve (keep the duck fat for other cooking, as it will have a delicious flavour).

When the beef has finished roasting, remove from the pan to a carving board and set aside to rest for 8-10 minutes in a warm place. Pour excess fat from the pan, then add the vegetables to the meat juices and toss over a moderately low heat to brown lightly. Season. Add the watercress leaves, if using, and toss to mix with the vegetables.

Place the beef rib so the bone is on one side. Cut the meat vertically and lengthways into slices. Spoon the vegetables on to the hot plates, arrange the slices of beef on top and sprinkle with a little coarse sea salt. Add a drizzle of aged vinegar round the edge and serve.

This dish has regularly featured on my menus through the years. It is a lovely way to cook rib of beef, which has a quality of meat that is finer than fillet. Giving balsamic vinegar this treatment makes it as mellow and flavourful as one that has been aged for 10 years or more.

Roasted veal sweetbreads with spinach and ceps

Serves 4

4 veal 'heart' sweetbreads (2 pairs),
(125-150 g each)
softened unsalted butter
sunflower oil
For the spinach with ceps
700 g fresh spinach, coarse
stalks discarded
unsalted butter

3 shallots, peeled and chopped
1 garlic clove, peeled and
finely chopped
300 g button mushrooms or fresh ceps,
trimmed and sliced
4 tablespoons double cream
freshly grated nutmeg
salt and freshly ground black pepper

Ask your butcher to prepare the sweetbreads for you. There is no need to blanch them – cooked this way they end up with a moist interior and a crisp outside.

Soak the sweetbreads overnight in cold water to extract any blood.

Preheat the oven to 250°C or its highest setting.

To prepare the spinach, add it gradually to a large pan of boiling salted water (or blanch in 2 batches). As soon as the water returns to the boil, drain and refresh with cold water. When the spinach is cool enough to handle, squeeze it in handfuls to remove excess moisture. Coarsely chop and set aside.

Drain the sweetbreads and dry them thoroughly with kitchen paper. Remove the fat and skin, leaving the membrane that holds them together. Season all over, then brush with softened butter. Heat enough sunflower oil for shallow frying in a heavy-based pan with an ovenproof handle. Put the sweetbreads into the pan, presentation side down first, and cook over a high heat to sear and brown until crisp. Turn the sweetbreads over and put into the oven. Cook for 6-7 minutes, basting twice with the fat in the pan.

Meanwhile, finish the spinach. Melt a knob of butter in a heavy-based pan and sweat the shallots and garlic until soft. Add the ceps or mushrooms and cook over a moderate heat until they start giving off their juice. Add the cream and stir, then bring to the boil. Add the spinach and mix in thoroughly. Season to taste with nutmeg, salt and pepper. Keep hot.

Remove the sweetbreads with tongs to kitchen paper to drain off excess fat. Season them lightly.

To serve, spoon the spinach and ceps in the centre of hot plates and set a sweetbread on top of each.

Roast chicken with savoury bread pudding and tarragon

Serves 4

1 organic free-range chicken
  (about 1.5 kg)
1 lemon, halved
fresh thyme
softened unsalted butter
1 glass of white wine
1 tablespoon chopped fresh tarragon
For the bread pudding
450 ml milk
1 small bay leaf
1 sprig of fresh thyme

1 garlic clove, peeled and crushed
2 whole cloves
grated zest of $\frac{1}{2}$ lemon
freshly grated nutmeg
unsalted butter
150 g white bread, crust removed
  and broken up
1 small onion, peeled and very
  finely chopped
1 egg + 2 egg whites
salt and freshly ground black pepper

To make the bread puddings, put the milk, bay leaf, thyme, garlic, cloves, lemon zest and a little nutmeg in a saucepan, and heat until bubbles form round the edge of the pan. Remove from the heat and set aside to infuse for 20 minutes.

Meanwhile, prepare the moulds. Brush all over the inside of four chilled dariole moulds with a thin layer of melted butter, then return to the fridge or freezer to chill until the butter has set. Brush with another layer of melted butter and chill again.

Put the bread in a bowl, strain over the flavoured milk and leave to soak for 20 minutes.

Preheat the oven to 180°C/gas mark 4.

I hate bread sauce, but made into a pudding like this it is great – amazing what a different consistency can do. In the restaurant we serve the puddings with sautéed chicken breasts. The chicken is delicious with spinach and roast parsnips, and carrots. If you want the sauce to have a gravy consistency, you can thicken it with a little cornflour or arrowroot.

To prepare the chicken for roasting, set it in a small roasting tin or dish. Squeeze the juice from one lemon half over the bird and put the squeezed half inside the body cavity with some thyme. Truss the bird by tying the wingtips to the knuckle joints on the legs. Spread softened butter all over the bird, then sprinkle with more thyme (leaves and/or flowertips).

Put the chicken into the oven and roast for 1½-1¾ hours, basting with the juices in the tin from time to time. To test if the chicken is cooked, pierce the meaty part of the thigh with the tip of a sharp knife – the juices that run out should be clear.

Meanwhile, finish the bread puddings. Melt a small knob of butter in a pan and sweat the onion until very soft but not coloured. Add to the soaked bread. Lightly beat the egg with the egg whites and add to the bowl. Mix together thoroughly and season. Spoon into the buttered dariole moulds. Set the moulds on a layer of folded newspaper in a small roasting tin and pour hot water into the tin to come half way up the sides of the moulds.

Put into the oven with the chicken to bake for 1 hour.

When the chicken has finished cooking, put it on a carving board and set aside in a warm place to rest for 15 minutes. Skim off some of the fat from the juices in the tin. Set the tin over a moderate heat, add the wine and bring to the boil, stirring to deglaze. Strain into a small saucepan and bring back to the boil. Check the seasoning, then add a squeeze of lemon juice and the tarragon. Keep hot.

Carve the chicken and divide among the hot plates. Turn out the bread puddings and put one on each plate. Moisten the chicken and puddings with the sauce and serve.

Roast squab pigeon with garlic confit

Serves 4

4 squab pigeons

For the garlic confit

2 whole garlic bulbs, separated into
   cloves and peeled

100 g unsalted butter, melted

a few sprigs of fresh thyme

½ bay leaf

For the celeriac and potato mash

1 head celeriac

milk and water for cooking

1 medium-sized floury potato

salt and freshly ground pepper

To prepare the pigeons for cooking, remove the wishbone, then spatchcock the birds (cut down both sides of the backbone and remove it, then flatten the birds). Trim off excess ribcage. Set aside.

For the garlic confit, put the garlic cloves in a saucepan and cover with the melted butter. Add the thyme, bay leaf, and salt and pepper to taste. Cook gently for 15-20 minutes to soften the garlic but not colour it. Remove from the heat and set aside.

Preheat the oven to 220°C/gas mark 7.

To make the mash, peel the celeriac and cut into equal-size small pieces. As they are cut, drop them into a pan of cold milk and water (half and half). Peel the potato and cut into pieces the same size as the celeriac. Add to the pan. If necessary, add more milk and water so that the vegetables are generously covered. Bring to the boil, then reduce the heat and simmer for 10-15 minutes or until just tender.

Meanwhile, season the pigeons and brush them on both sides with the garlic-flavoured butter. Heat a heavy-based pan that can also be put into the oven. Put the pigeons in the pan, skin side down, and sear for 1½-2 minutes or until browned. Turn the birds over and brown the other side. Turn back on to the skin side, then put into the oven to roast for 8 minutes (the meat will be rosy-pink). When the pigeons have finished roasting, remove them from the oven and set aside in a warm place to rest for 7 minutes.

Drain the celeriac and potato in a colander set in a bowl, then mash coarsely with a potato masher or fork. If the mash is too dry, moisten with a little of the cooking liquid. Season to taste and keep hot.

Place the pigeons on a chopping board, skin side down (reserve the juices in the roasting pan). Using a small knife, remove the breast meat from the bone; discard the breast bone and rib cage. Season the pigeon joints. Place on warmed plates and keep hot.

Remove the garlic cloves from the garlic-flavoured butter using a slotted spoon, and brown them quickly in a hot pan. Scatter the garlic round the pigeons. Add a spoonful of the celeriac mash to each plate, shaped into a quenelle if you like. Make a little well in the mash and put in the pigeon roasting juices. Serve.

A coarse celeriac and potato mash is given here, to serve with the pigeon, but you could also serve the birds with the roasted root vegetables in the rib of beef recipe on page 126. Be sure you use youngish garlic for the confit – some garlic can be 2 years old.

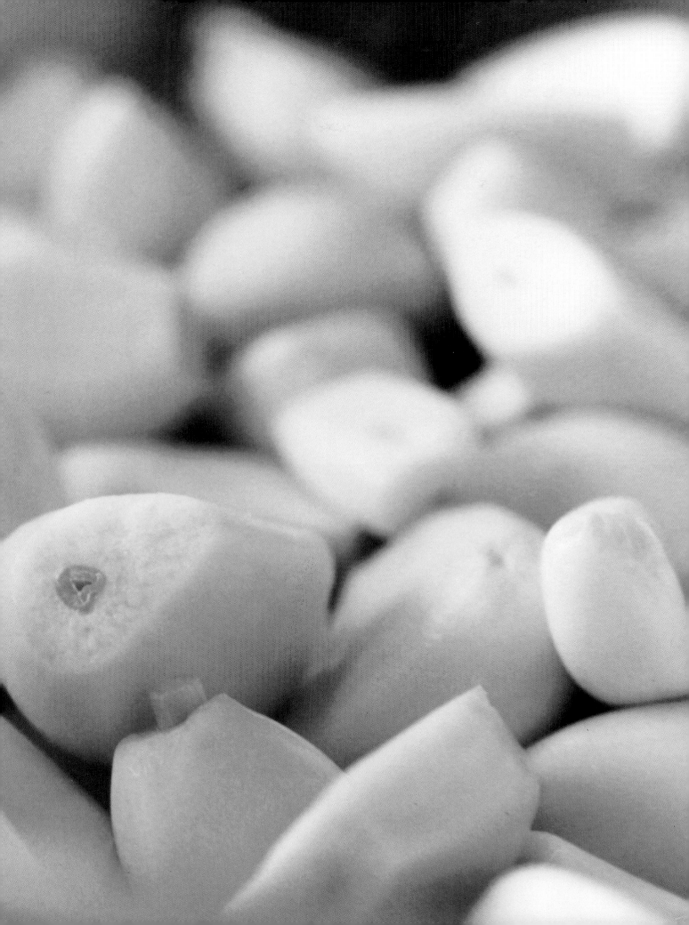

Pan-roasted carrots and parsnips

Serves 4

350 g medium carrots
350 g medium parsnips
duck fat or garlic-flavoured butter
  (see garlic confit, page 132)
1 bunch of watercress, coarse
  stalks discarded
salt and freshly ground black pepper

Peel the carrots and parsnips, and cut into slices about 2 cm thick. Drop into a saucepan of boiling salted water and blanch for 2 minutes. Drain and refresh.

Heat a film of duck fat or garlic-flavoured butter in a large heavy-based pan. Season the carrots and parsnips, then add to the pan. Brown over a brisk heat, then reduce the heat and continue cooking until tender. (Alternatively, if the oven is on, you can transfer the vegetables to the oven to finish cooking.)

Drain off excess fat, then toss the carrots and parsnips with the watercress (plus any meat juices you might have from roasting). Check the seasoning and serve hot.

Adding the watercress at the end means that it wilts only slightly and keeps its peppery crunch.

Baked field mushrooms

Serves 4

8 medium-sized field mushrooms
3 garlic cloves, peeled and very
thinly sliced
8 small sprigs of fresh marjoram
good olive oil
coarse sea salt
freshly ground pepper

You can also prepare portobello mushrooms or cultivated large open-cap mushrooms in the same way.

Preheat the oven to 220°C/gas mark 7.

Peel the mushroom caps and trim the stalks. Arrange the caps, gill side up, in an oiled roasting tin. Give each mushroom a generous sprinkling of coarse salt and pepper, a few slices of garlic and a sprig of marjoram. Finish with a sprinkling of olive oil.

Bake for 15-20 minutes.

Turnip and potato gratin

Serves 4

8 slices Parma ham, cut into
    fine shreds
400 g large turnips, peeled
250 g waxy potatoes, peeled

160 ml double cream
40 ml milk
100 g Gruyère, grated
salt and freshly ground black pepper

Preheat the oven to 170°C/gas mark 3. Preheat the grill.

    Grill the shreds of Parma ham until crisp. Set aside.

    Thinly slice the turnips and potatoes on a mandoline – you want slices no more than 3 mm thick. Put them into two bowls, keeping the turnips and potatoes separate. Season both with salt and pepper.

    Warm the cream and milk in a small saucepan. Add half of the hot mixture to each bowl and turn the vegetables to moisten them (the easiest way to do this is with your fingers).

    Butter a gratin dish that is about 4 cm deep. Make a layer of turnip slices on the bottom, then cover with half of the potato slices. Sprinkle over a layer of Gruyère and then Parma ham. Repeat the layers to fill the dish. Pour the remainder of the cream mixture over the top and finish with a sprinkling of the last of the cheese.

    Set the gratin dish in a roasting tin of water (bain marie) and cover with foil. Bake for 45 minutes or until the potato and turnip slices are tender. Remove the foil and bake for a further 20 minutes to brown the top. Serve hot.

Turnips have no starch, so to make a gratin they need to be combined with potatoes. Otherwise, the gratin would fall asunder.

Mashed potatoes

Serves 6
1 kg floury potatoes
150 g salted butter
250 ml creamy milk
salt and white pepper

You need good floury potatoes for mash, such as Golden Wonder or King Edwards. This may seem a lot of potatoes, but to an Irishman you can't have too many spuds.

Put the potatoes, in their skins, in a big pan of cold salted water and bring to the boil. Reduce the heat and simmer for about 20 minutes or until the potatoes are tender but not mushy. Drain, then return to the pan, off the heat. Cover the pan with a folded tea towel – or an old newspaper, which is what my mother always used – and leave for 5-10 minutes so the potatoes can steam off the excess moisture.

Meanwhile, put the butter and milk in another pan and heat until the milk has bubbles round the edge and the butter has melted. Remove from the heat and keep warm.

Uncover the pan of potatoes and, when they are cool enough to handle, peel them. Put them through a potato ricer or mouli-légumes, or mash by hand with a potato masher. Add the hot butter and milk, and mix in with a wooden spoon. Season to taste.

Fig tart with vanilla ice-cream and tobacco syrup

Serves 8

500 g fresh puff pastry
frangipane (see Banana tart, page 50)
6-8 ripe but firm figs
icing sugar
Vanilla ice-cream for serving
  (see page 202)

For the tobacco syrup

1 packet (12.5 g) Old Holborn tobacco
20 g sugar
5 teaspoons arrowroot mixed with
  1 tablespoon cold water

Roll out the puff pastry until very thin (about 3 mm). Cut out 13 cm discs and set them on baking trays lined with greaseproof paper. Using your thumb and index finger and the back, blunt edge of a knife, crimp the edge of each disc to make a rim. Prick the centre of each disc all over with a fork. Set aside in the fridge to rest for 20-30 minutes.

Meanwhile, make the tobacco syrup. Bring 400 ml water to the boil in a small saucepan. Put half of the tobacco in a bowl and pour over the boiling water. Leave to infuse for 3 minutes. Strain through a fine sieve back into the saucepan, then add the sugar and stir to dissolve. Add the arrowroot mixture and bring to the boil, stirring until thickened. Add a tiny pinch of the remaining tobacco – just a few strands. Remove from the heat and set aside to cool.

Preheat the oven to 200°C/gas mark 6.

Spoon the frangipane on to the centre of the pastry discs and spread out to make a mound about 6 mm thick, leaving 1.5 cm of the pastry uncovered all round. Very thinly slice each fig horizontally (about 2 mm thick). Reserve a few slices for the top of the tarts, then fan the remainder out around the frangipane, leaning them on to it slightly and curving all the way round. The slices should slightly overlap. Cover the top of the

frangipane with the reserved fig slices, overlapping them.

Dust the fig slices generously with icing sugar, then bake the tarts for about 20 minutes or until the figs are caramelized and shiny and the pastry rim is puffed and golden.

To serve, set a tart on each plate and top with a scoop of vanilla ice-cream. Drizzle round the tobacco syrup.

Since I first put tobacco syrup on the menu at Lindsay House it has been a talking point. The fig tarts are also delicious with spiced bread ice-cream (see page 202), and a drizzle of warmed honey mixed with a squeeze of lemon juice instead of the tobacco syrup.

Spiced madeleines with lemon curd and apricot-orange compote

Serves 6

For the spiced madeleines

30 g sultanas

15 g plain flour

75 g caster sugar

15 g ground almonds

½ teaspoon ground ginger

½ teaspoon ground cinnamon

½ teaspoon ground liquorice

large pinch of ground mace

large pinch of Chinese five-spice
    powder

large pinch of freshly grated nutmeg

65 g unsalted butter

1 tablespoon clear honey, such as acacia

2 egg whites

icing sugar to dust

For the lemon curd

1 egg + 1 egg yolk

50 g caster sugar

grated zest and juice of 1 lemon

60 g cold unsalted butter, diced

100 ml whipping cream

For the compote

6 ripe apricots, halved and stoned

about 150 ml white wine

caster sugar to taste

3 oranges

For the madeleines, put the sultanas into a saucepan, cover with water and bring to the boil. Remove from the heat and leave to soak overnight to plump up. Drain and set aside.

To make the lemon curd, put the egg, yolk, sugar, and lemon zest and juice in a bain marie (the top of a double saucepan or in a heatproof bowl set over a pan of simmering water). Stir until the sugar dissolves then continue cooking gently, stirring frequently, until the mixture has thickened. This will take 10-20 minutes. Do not let the mixture boil. Remove from the heat and whisk in the cold butter until melted. Leave to cool to room temperature. Whip the cream and fold into the curd. Cover and keep in the fridge until ready to serve.

Mix together all the dry ingredients for the madeleines in a bowl. Melt the butter in a small saucepan and cook until it turns nut brown (the colour of hazelnut shells). Remove from the heat and stir in the honey. Allow to cool slightly, then add to the dry ingredients. Beat together using an electric mixer. Gradually add the egg whites, mixing them in. The consistency of the mixture should be like a runny choux pastry. Cover and chill for at least 30 minutes. At the same time, chill a 12-mould madeleine sheet.

Meanwhile, for the compote, put the apricots in a small saucepan and just cover with white wine. Add sugar to sweeten to taste and bring to the boil. Simmer gently for 4 minutes. Remove from the heat and leave the apricots to cool in the syrup.

Preheat the oven to 170°C/gas mark 3. Brush a thin layer of melted butter all over the inside of the madeleine moulds, then return to the fridge or freezer to chill until

Instead of lemon curd, you could serve the madeleines with the mascarpone mousse on page 99 or just with sweetened crème fraîche. The white wine used to poach the apricots can be added to the syrup for the drunken fruits on page 192.

the butter has set. Brush with another layer of melted butter, then dust with flour and shake out excess.

Scatter the sultanas over the bottom of the prepared moulds (6-8 in each one). Spoon the mixture into the moulds and bake for 10-15 minutes or until golden brown and just firm to the touch.

Meanwhile, peel and segment the oranges. Add to the apricots in syrup and stir to mix.

When the madeleines have finished baking, remove them from the oven and allow to cool slightly in the tins. Then gently ease them out.

To serve, put 2 warm madeleines on each plate and dust them with icing sugar. Add a quenelle of lemon curd to each plate. Use a slotted spoon to lift the apricots and orange segments out of the syrup and on to the plates.

Saffron rice pudding with prune syrup

Serves 6

For the prune syrup

200 g stoned Agen prunes
(preferably not ready-to-eat)

hot, strong, unscented tea

100 g sugar

2 tablespoons armagnac

For the pudding

750 ml full-cream milk

200 ml double cream

a good pinch of saffron strands

90 g short-grain pudding rice

50 g unsalted butter

70 g caster sugar

grated zest of 1 orange

1 vanilla pod, split open

coarsely crushed pistachios to finish

This is a sort of Moorish (definitely more-ish) version of an English favourite. The pudding can also be served at room temperature, in which case you may need to thin it down a little with milk. A thin, crisp biscuit is a good accompaniment.

For the prune syrup, cover the prunes with hot tea and leave to soak and plump up overnight.

The next day, dissolve the sugar in 100 ml water. Bring to the boil, then remove from the heat. Drain the prunes and add to the hot syrup. Stir in the armagnac. Leave to cool to room temperature.

To make the pudding, put the milk and cream in a heavy-based saucepan and add the saffron. Heat until bubbles appear round the edge, then add the rice, butter, sugar and orange zest. Scrape the tiny seeds out of the vanilla pod into the mixture, and add the pod too. Bring to the boil, stirring, then reduce the heat to the lowest setting (use a heat diffuser if you have one). Cook for about 45 minutes, stirring frequently, until the rice is tender and the pudding is creamy. Remove the vanilla pod.

To serve, ladle the hot rice pudding into soup bowls and spoon the prunes in syrup around or on top. Finish with a sprinkling of crushed pistachios.

Apple and cobnut crumble

Serves 6-8

For the filling

60 g sultanas

50 g light soft brown sugar

½ teaspoon ground cinnamon

¼ teaspoon ground cloves

juice of ¼ lemon

good dash of Calvados

800 g cooking apples such as Bramleys

For the crumble topping

150 g wholemeal flour

75 g unsalted butter, chilled

75 g light soft brown sugar

50 g cobnuts removed from husks,
    chopped

1 teaspoon ground cinnamon

Combine the sultanas, sugar, spices, lemon juice and Calvados in a saucepan and heat gently just to warm the mixture, stirring to dissolve the sugar. Remove from the heat and leave to macerate for 2-3 hours.

Preheat the oven to 180°C/gas mark 4.

To make the topping, put the flour in a bowl and rub in the butter until the mixture resembles fine breadcrumbs. Add the sugar, cobnuts and cinnamon, and stir to mix.

Peel and core the apples, then chop them into small chunks, all about the same size. Put them into a pie dish or other baking dish of about 2 litre capacity and pour over the sultana mixture. Stir together. Scatter the topping mixture evenly over the top. Bake for about 45 minutes or until the apples are tender and the topping is crisp. Serve hot.

You can, of course, use hazelnuts instead of cobnuts, and a mixture of plain white and wholemeal flours (half and half) if you prefer. Serve this in traditional style, with a good egg custard (see page 194).

Marinated pumpkin with chocolate sorbet

Serves 8

about 450 g pumpkin, in one piece
250 ml freshly squeezed orange juice
2 pieces of stem ginger in syrup, sliced
2 teaspoons arrowroot mixed with
   2 teaspoons cold water
caster sugar to taste
coarsely crushed pistachios to garnish
Chocolate tuiles (see page 205)
   for serving

For the chocolate sorbet

100 ml milk
150 g caster sugar
2 tablespoons liquid glucose
20 g cocoa powder
100 g dark chocolate, preferably
   Valrhona or a good Belgian
   chocolate, chopped

Remove the skin and seeds from the pumpkin, then weigh the flesh. You need 250 g, in one piece. Use a vegetable peeler to cut ribbons from the pumpkin, cutting lengthways down the cut side of the piece, not the back or the curved front. Put the orange juice in a saucepan with 150 ml water and add the ginger. Bring to the boil. Add the pumpkin strips and simmer gently until they are tender but still firm (like al dente pasta). Remove with a slotted spoon and spread out on a tray in one layer to cool.

This was inspired by a Turkish dish of pumpkin in syrup with green walnuts. You must use a ripe French pumpkin for this, not one that is woody or fibrous.

Boil the cooking liquid until reduced to about 300 ml. Remove from the heat and leave to cool slightly, then stir in the arrowroot mixture. Bring back to the boil, stirring until thickened. Remove from the heat and leave to cool. Taste the syrup and add sugar to sweeten, stirring until dissolved.

Lay out 3 strips of pumpkin on the work surface, end to end. Roll up, not too tightly. Continue making rolls in this way, then pack them into a container side by side, standing upright. Pour in the syrup, which should just cover the pumpkin rolls. Leave to marinate overnight.

To make the chocolate sorbet, put the milk, sugar, glucose and cocoa powder in a saucepan with 400 ml water. Bring to the boil, stirring to dissolve the sugar, then remove from the heat. Add the chocolate and stir until it has melted. Leave to cool, then chill until cold. Pour into an ice-cream machine and freeze. Once softly frozen, transfer to a freezerproof container and put into the freezer to 'mature' for an hour or so. If freezing for longer than 1 hour, transfer the sorbet to the fridge 20 minutes before serving to soften slightly. (The sorbet is best if made on the day of serving.)

To serve, put a scoop of sorbet in the centre of each plate. Lift the pumpkin rolls carefully out of the container and arrange 3 round the sorbet on each plate. Drizzle the pumpkin syrup over the pumpkin rolls, sprinkle with pistachios and add a chocolate tuile or two.

Autumn wine

Food and wine are bound by the same mutual respect. When we speak of matching them we look for correlations that are climatic, seasonal, cultural, even spiritual. Although terroir is an idea, and as such not solely the province of the French, it is generally true that regional wines from France are philosophically in tune with the style of earthy native cooking that may be termed British.

Autumn is the time of harvests and festivals, of grapes maturing on the vines through misty mornings and long golden afternoons, and of wild westerly winds, mulching leaves and odours of humus. The massively aromatic grape varieties from Alsace are now being harvested, to yield extraordinary rich, creamy wines, gravid with orchard fruit and exotic spice flavours, wines that are meant to be drunk with food. Tokay Pinot Gris is fabulous with lightly curried dishes and those dressed with cream or butter; the Rieslings from Alsace and Germany might have been invented for the local choucroute (sauerkraut). Condrieu from the Rhône certainly has the weight to go with meaty white fish such as monkfish and the necessary candied sweetness to accompany offal like sweetbreads. Also good with foie gras or terrine would be a late-harvested Gewürztraminer or sweet Jurançon. Sweet whites with body and clean acidity can work with a range of different foods, from scallops to pork to cheese.

The comparatively neglected rustic wines of Gascony, flavoursome, earthy, herbal and almost medicinal, complement roasted dishes such as pigeon and rib of beef. These wines are 'gravy' to meat. Italian nebbiolo, old Rhônes and, especially, vintage Pinot Noir, with its pronounced vegetal character, can accompany the wonderful wild mushrooms that grow in our damp climate.

This is the time of year to mix and match creatively, to experiment boldly with flavours (try vintage Banyuls, a savoury-sweet wine from the Roussillon, with braised hare, for example). It is also the season to sample some glorious sweet wines, which are a dessert in themselves: a Beerenauslese from Austria, a rich Tokaji from Hungary or any wine affected by noble rot, the benevolent bacterium that concentrates the sugars in the grapes and gives rise to Sauternes, the great Rieslings from the Rhine and the marvellous Loire nectars.

Douglas Wregg

Autumn cheese

For most sheep or goat herds and some cow herds which have a natural cycle of lactation, autumn is the end of the cycle. The milk can be very rich, as the animal produces less volume and more concentration. This is a wonderful time of year for many cheeses, particularly hard sheep and goat's milk cheeses:

Ticklemore
Spenwood
Berkswell
Tyning

Most of the cheeses made in the autumn will be ready to eat the following year (and up to a year later). Stilton made in September and October becomes the delicious cheese we enjoy at Christmas.

Randolph Hodgson, Neal's Yard Dairy

the heavy steps of
the ploughman splashing
the wintry mould

winter

best in winter

cod **plaice** lemon sole **halibut** herring **mackerel** sprats **mullet** scallops
hare rabbit **venison** grouse **partridge** pheasant **pigeon** quail **snipe**
wild goose **wild duck** woodcock **cabbages** Brussels sprouts **broccoli**
cauliflower **leeks** parsnips **celeriac** endive **celery** apples **pears**
forced rhubarb **citrus fruits** dried fruits **nuts**

Lentil and wild rabbit soup

Serves 6-8

1 wild rabbit, jointed
2 carrots, peeled and halved
1 onion, peeled and halved
2 celery sticks, trimmed and halved
about 1.5 litres chicken stock
1 garlic clove, peeled and halved
2 juniper berries, bruised

5-6 black peppercorns
1 large fresh bouquet garni of parsley, thyme and bay leaf
200 g dried Puy lentils, rinsed
125 ml full-bodied red wine
125 ml port
salt and freshly ground black pepper

Wild rabbit and lentils have a natural affinity. This is a hearty soup with an earthy flavour. Serve it with croutons or toasted bread.

Put the rabbit and vegetables in a large pot and cover generously with chicken stock. Bring to the boil, skimming off any scum. Add the garlic, juniper berries, peppercorns and bouquet garni. Reduce the heat and simmer for 30 minutes.

Lift out the rabbit joints and set aside to cool slightly. Strain the stock and return to the pan. Bring back to the boil. Add the lentils and simmer for 20 minutes or until tender.

Meanwhile, remove the meat from the rabbit joints and shred it coarsely. Keep warm.

Put the wine and port in a small pan and boil until reduced to about 5 tablespoons. Add to the lentils just before they have finished cooking.

Transfer the lentil mixture to a food processor and purée. Pour back into the pan. If too thick, add some chicken stock or water. Reheat, then check the seasoning.

Put the shredded rabbit in soup bowls and ladle over the hot lentil soup. Serve immediately.

Irish spiced beef

1 joint of topside of beef
(about 2.7 kg), tied without fat
1 large celery stick, trimmed and
roughly chopped
1 large carrot, peeled and roughly chopped
1 onion, peeled and roughly chopped
1 garlic clove, peeled
3 whole cloves
1 bay leaf
good mustard or horseradish
sauce for serving
For the brine
450 g sea salt

15 g saltpetre (optional)
1 large carrot, peeled and diced
1 celery stick, trimmed and diced
1 fresh red chilli, chopped
4 garlic cloves, peeled and chopped
225 g demerara sugar
1 tablespoon juniper berries,
lightly broken
1 tablespoon black peppercorns,
lightly broken
1 tablespoon coriander seeds,
lightly broken
1 bottle (75 cl) red wine

The beef can also be served hot, with baby beetroots and leeks. As a main course it will serve about 12. A good butcher who salts his own meat may sell you a small quantity of saltpetre, or you can omit it.

Combine all the ingredients for the brine in a non-reactive saucepan and add 500 ml of water. Bring to the boil, stirring to dissolve the salt and sugar. Remove from the heat and leave until cold.

Put the joint of beef in a large bowl. Pour over the brine and cover. Leave in the fridge for 4-5 days, turning the beef regularly.

Drain the beef, discarding the brine, and put it in a large pot. Add the vegetables, garlic, cloves and bay leaf and cover with fresh cold water. Bring to the boil, then cover, reduce the heat and simmer for 3½ hours or until the beef is tender. Turn it over from time to time, and top up with boiling water if necessary. Remove from the heat and leave to cool in the liquid.

Remove the beef when it is cold. Cut it into very thin slices and serve with good mustard or horseradish sauce and bread.

Crisp-fried crubeens with tartare sauce

Serves 6-8

6 pig's trotters, well cleaned and
hairs removed
vegetable stock, or water with
vegetables (coarsely chopped onion,
carrot, celery and leek) and a
bouquet garni to flavour
2 eggs
2 tablespoons milk
120 g fine fresh breadcrumbs
1 teaspoon dry mustard
seasoned flour
sunflower oil

For the butcher's brine

900 g sea salt
450 g light soft brown sugar
1 tablespoon saltpetre (optional)

1 whole clove
10 black peppercorns
6 juniper berries
4 garlic cloves, peeled and split in half
1 bay leaf
3 sprigs of fresh thyme

For the tartare sauce

1 egg + 2 egg yolks
2 teaspoons Dijon mustard
about 2 tablespoons white wine vinegar
salt and freshly ground black pepper
300 ml salad oil, such as sunflower
1 1/2 tablespoons finely chopped capers
1 1/2 tablespoons finely chopped gherkins
1 1/2 tablespoons finely chopped onion
1 1/2 tablespoons finely chopped parsley

First make the brine. Put all the ingredients in a pan with 3 litres water and bring to the boil, stirring until the sugar dissolves and skimming off the foam with a slotted spoon. Simmer for 10 minutes, then remove from the heat and leave to cool.

Put the trotters in a large bowl and pour over the cold brine. Cover the trotters with a plate to keep them submerged, then cover the bowl and put into the refrigerator. Leave for 24 hours.

Drain the trotters (discard the brine) and put them in a pot. Cover with vegetable stock, or with water and the flavouring vegetables and bouquet garni. Bring to a simmer, skimming well, then cover and leave to cook gently for about 3½ hours or until the meat starts to come away from the bones. Top up with boiling water if necessary. Remove from the heat and leave the trotters to cool in the stock. (In Ireland, crubeens are most often eaten warm, straight from the stock.)

When cool enough to handle, drain the trotters. Split each one down the middle and take out all the bones. Leave the gristle, if you like, as it makes good eating too. Put the halves back together and wrap each trotter tightly in cling film. Chill for half a day – the gelatine in the trotters will solidify and bind them back together.

To make the tartare sauce, put the egg, yolks, mustard, 1 tablespoon vinegar and

Crubeens – or *crúbíní* – are a traditional Irish delicacy. I like to cure the trotters in a butcher's brine before cooking them, to add flavour and improve the colour. Jane Grigson gives a similar brine in her book *English Food*, where she points out that saltpetre gives brined meat 'an appetising rosy colour'. Saltpetre is not easy to find these days, but do try to get some as it really makes a difference.

a little salt and pepper in a bowl and whisk together until thick. Start adding the oil, drop by drop at first, whisking constantly. When about 2 tablespoons of oil have been added, the rest can be poured in in a slow stream, still whisking. Add the remaining vinegar. Stir in the capers, gherkins, onion and parsley. Taste and add more vinegar, salt and pepper if needed. Cover and keep in a cool place or the refrigerator until ready to serve.

Unwrap the trotters and cut them across into slices about 2 cm thick. Lightly beat the eggs with the milk in a shallow dish. Mix the breadcrumbs with the mustard in another dish. Dredge the slices of trotter in seasoned flour, then dip in the eggs and, finally, coat with the crumbs. Shallow fry in hot sunflower oil until golden brown and crisp on both sides. Drain on kitchen paper and serve hot, with the tartare sauce.

Cream of mussel soup with beef marrow quenelles

Serves 4

unsalted butter

4 shallots, peeled and finely chopped

2 garlic cloves, peeled and chopped

1 kg mussels, preferably rope-grown,
   scrubbed and debearded

250 ml dry white wine

a few parsley stalks

a few white peppercorns, coarsely
   crushed

about 500 ml chicken stock

2 tablespoons cornflour mixed with
   4 tablespoons water

250 ml double cream

chopped fresh chives and chervil
   to garnish

For the quenelles

115 g beef bone marrow

1 teaspoon each chopped fresh
   parsley and chervil

115 g dried white breadcrumbs

3 egg yolks

1 teaspoon cornflour

salt and freshly ground white pepper

First make the quenelle mixture. Put all the ingredients in a food processor with some seasoning and blend until smooth and well mixed. Scoop into a bowl, cover and chill while you make the soup.

Melt a little knob of butter in a heavy-based pan and sweat the shallots and garlic until softened. Add the mussels, wine, parsley stalks and peppercorns. Cover and steam for 3-5 minutes, shaking the pan frequently, until the mussel shells open. Discard any mussels that remain stubbornly closed. Remove from the heat and leave to cool a little, still covered.

This would normally be thickened with a liaison of cream and egg yolks, but using a starch thickening instead there is no danger of the soup curdling. If you don't want to make the quenelles, the soup is very good without them.

Turn the mussels into a colander set in a bowl to drain. Shell the mussels and set aside, adding any juices from the shells to the cooking liquid in the bowl. Strain the cooking liquid through muslin, and make it up to 700 ml with chicken stock. Pour into a clean pan. Add the cornflour mixture and bring to the boil, stirring until thickened. Add the cream and season to taste.

Shape the marrow mixture into small quenelles using two teaspoons or shape into small balls. Add to the simmering soup and poach for 5-6 minutes. Add the shelled mussels and reheat briefly.

Serve in a soup tureen, garnished with chopped chives and chervil.

Cod with cockles

Serves 4

1 kg cockles

4 cod steaks with skin, about

2 cm thick

sunflower oil

25 g unsalted butter

1 teaspoon chopped fresh dill

1 teaspoon snipped fresh chives

lemon juice

225 g young spinach leaves

olive oil

salt and freshly ground black pepper

Be sure your cockles come from a good source, otherwise they will be very sandy. Once sand is in the shells, it is very hard to get it out. I suggest this be served in soup plates so that you can enjoy all the lovely cockle juices as a broth, although you can serve on plates and spoon over only a little of the juice if you prefer.

Put the cockles in a basin of cold water and leave to purge for a day, stirring every few hours. This will help to clean out any sand from the shells.

Preheat the oven to 200°C/gas mark 6.

Season the cod steaks. Heat a film of sunflower oil in a wide, heavy-based pan. Put the cod steaks in the hot pan and brown lightly on both sides. Transfer to a heavy baking tray and bake for 15 minutes. When cooked the central bone in each steak should be able to be removed if pulled gently.

Meanwhile, drain and rinse the cockles, and put into a hot pan. Add no liquid as the cockle juices are very delicate in flavour. Cover and steam over a moderately high heat for about 5 minutes or until the shells open, shaking the pan occasionally.

Tip the cockles into a colander set in a bowl. Remove them from their shells – adding all the juices to the bowl – and keep warm in a separate bowl. Strain the juices in the bowl through muslin into a saucepan. Reheat gently, then add the butter. Tilt the pan to swirl the butter into the sauce. Add the dill and chives, and a squeeze of lemon juice. Check the seasoning and keep hot.

Dress the spinach with olive oil and a little lemon juice, and put a pile in the centre of each soup plate. Skin and bone the cod steaks, and set on the spinach. Spoon over the cockle juices, top with the cockles and serve.

Irish stew

Serves 4

2 middle necks of lamb, filleted, boned
   and bones reserved
450 g floury potatoes, such as
   King Edward, peeled
450 g waxy potatoes, such as Pentland
   Javelin or Maris Peer, peeled

700 g carrots, peeled
1 onion, peeled and thickly sliced
good pinch of fresh thyme leaves
salt and freshly ground black pepper
chopped fresh chives and parsley
   to garnish

When the butcher bones the lamb for you, have him give you the bones too. Make a well-flavoured stock using the bones and the trimmings from the carrots and onion, plus other vegetables and herbs you like. You need about 900 ml of lamb stock.

Cut the lamb into large chunks and put in a heavy-based saucepan. Pour in the stock. Bring to the boil, skimming off all the impurities from the surface. Remove the pieces of lamb with a draining spoon and reserve. Strain the stock through a fine sieve into a clean pan. Add the pieces of lamb and bring back to the boil. Reduce the heat, cover and simmer gently for 10 minutes.

Meanwhile, cut the carrots into pieces a little smaller than the pieces of lamb, and the potatoes into pieces the same size as the lamb. Add the carrots, onion and floury potatoes to the pan and simmer for another 10 minutes. Add the waxy potatoes and the thyme, and simmer for a further 15-20 minutes or until the lamb is very tender. The floury potatoes will have broken down to thicken the sauce, while the waxy potatoes will keep their shape.

Remove from the heat, cover and leave, without stirring, for 15 minutes.

Check the seasoning, then serve, sprinkled generously with chopped chives and parsley.

There is some controversy about whether carrots should be included in this dish. Escoffier says no, but then what would a Frenchman know about Irish stew? I like them. Cold pickled red cabbage is a traditional accompaniment in Ireland – you can use the recipe on page 204.

Daube of pork with dried apricots

Serves 4

sunflower oil

1 kg boned lean pork shoulder,
trimmed of all gristle and skin, cut
into large pieces about 8 cm square

12 whole dried apricots (not ready-
to-eat), stoned

100 ml white wine

200 ml orange juice

a little sugar to taste

about 350 ml brown meat stock

For the marinade

375 ml full-bodied red wine

250 ml olive oil

3-4 plum tomatoes, halved

6 garlic cloves, peeled and crushed

1 carrot, peeled and sliced

2 celery sticks, trimmed and chopped

1 leek, trimmed and sliced

1 onion, peeled and sliced

tiny pinch of cumin seeds

tiny pinch of fennel seeds

$1/2$ bunch of fresh mint, chopped

a few sprigs of fresh thyme

1 bay leaf

salt and freshly ground black pepper

Combine all the marinade ingredients in a big bowl.

Heat a film of sunflower oil in a heavy-based frying pan and fry the pork pieces until a rich dark brown on all sides. Drain and add to the marinade. Stir round, then cover and leave to marinate in the refrigerator for 24 hours.

Put the dried apricots, white wine, orange juice and a little sugar to sweeten in a saucepan and bring to the boil. Remove from the heat and leave to soak and rehydrate overnight.

The next day, preheat the oven to 180°C/gas mark 4.

Using a draining spoon, remove the pieces of pork from the marinade and transfer to a casserole. Pour the marinade into a saucepan and bring to the boil. Boil for 15 minutes, skimming off any foam from the surface. Add the stock, then pour over the meat in the casserole. Add more stock if the meat is not covered with liquid. Put on the

lid, or cover the casserole with foil, and put into the oven to cook for 2 hours.

Lift out the pieces of pork and reserve. Strain the cooking liquid through a fine sieve into a clean saucepan. If the liquid seems a bit thin, bring to the boil and boil to reduce. Check the seasoning. Drain the apricots and add to the sauce together with the pork. Heat through, then serve.

What a fine use for an economical cut of pork this is. Serve it with blanched shredded green cabbage tossed in butter. Delicious!

Saddle of rabbit with black pudding, roast vegetable and wild mushroom juice

Serves 4

For the rabbit

2 saddles of rabbit, with the livers
  and kidneys

200 g French black pudding

about 75 ml double cream

sunflower oil

1 shallot, peeled and chopped

1-2 garlic cloves, peeled and crushed

$^{1}/_{2}$ tablespoon chopped fresh thyme tips

8 thin slices of Bayonne ham or
  other good ham

4 sheets of caul fat, each about 25 cm
  square (about 300 g)

For the juice

2 tablespoons dry white wine

mirepoix of 2 tablespoons each
  chopped celery, carrot and onion

light stock or water

50 g peeled carrot, cut into small cubes

50 g peeled parsnip, cut into
  small cubes

50 g fresh wild mushrooms (preferably
  chanterelles), stalks trimmed
  and then sliced

To serve

400 g fresh spinach leaves, tough
  stalks discarded

12 Cornmeal cakes (see page 113)

salt and freshly ground black pepper

Have your butcher bone the saddles of rabbit, to yield 4 fillets. Ask him to chop the bones (which you want for the sauce).

To make the stuffing for the rabbit, take the black pudding from its skin and put into a food processor with the cream. Blend to a soft, spoonable consistency. Transfer to a bowl. Coarsely chop the rabbit livers and kidneys, and sauté in a little hot oil with the shallot and garlic just to sear and brown. Add the thyme for the last few seconds. Add the warm liver and kidney mixture to the black pudding and fold together. Check the seasoning.

Overlap 2 slices of ham on your work surface so that together they are the same length as a rabbit fillet. Lay a fillet on top and season with salt and pepper. Spread one-quarter of the black pudding mixture over the fillet. Fold the ham up over the stuffing, then roll up the rabbit fillet in the ham, rolling from a short end. Wrap the rolled rabbit in a sheet of caul fat and tie with kitchen string into a neat packet. (Do not tie too tightly as the black pudding filling will expand during cooking.) Make the remaining three rabbit packets in the same way. Set aside in the refrigerator.

Preheat the oven to 220°C/gas mark 7.

For the root vegetable and wild mushroom juice, heat a little oil in a saucepan. Add the mirepoix and rabbit bones (plus any vegetable and garlic trimmings) and cook to a good rich brown. Add the wine and boil until almost all evaporated. Pour in enough stock or water to cover the bones and vegetables. Bring to the boil and simmer for 15

This is, admittedly, a difficult recipe. If you are going to attempt it, it's worth doing it right and not leaving anything out because all the elements work so well together.

minutes, skimming regularly (if you skim constantly, you will end up with a beautifully clear liquid, not a cloudy one). Strain, preferably through a sieve lined with muslin. Keep this juice warm.

To cook the rabbit, brush the packets on all sides with oil, then put into a hot cast-iron frying pan that has an ovenproof handle. Cook over a moderate to low heat to sear to a golden brown on all sides. Transfer to the hot oven and cook for 5-8 minutes. Remove and leave to rest in a warm place while you finish the other components of the dish.

To finish the root vegetable and mushroom juice, heat a film of oil in a frying pan until very hot, then add the carrot and parsnip cubes and the sliced mushrooms and toss for 2½-3 minutes. Drain on kitchen paper, then add to the warm juice. Check the seasoning.

For the spinach, toss the leaves in a hot pan until they are wilted and juices are exuded. Drain well and season. Keep hot.

To serve, cut each rabbit packet into three slices. Set three cornmeal cakes on each plate, pile spinach on top and arrange the rabbit on the spinach. Add all the juices from the rabbit to the root vegetable and mushroom juice, and spoon over the rabbit.

Mallard with pineapple and pak choi

Serves 4

2 mallards (about 2 kg each)

duck or goose fat

8 baby pak choi

salt and freshly ground black pepper

2 garlic cloves, peeled and finely
chopped

sunflower oil

1 small ripe pineapple

caster sugar

$^1/_2$ teaspoon very finely chopped
fresh red chilli

For the spiced salt

1 tablespoon coarse rock salt

1 tablespoon five-spice powder

1 tablespoon juniper berries

1 tablespoon fresh thyme leaves

1 tablespoon cayenne pepper

1 dried bay leaf

2 garlic cloves, peeled

For the sauce

3-4 limes

$^1/_2$ teaspoon finely chopped fresh ginger

1 tablespoon caster sugar

100 ml chicken or veal stock

2 teaspoons cornflour mixed with
2 teaspoons cold water

First make the spiced salt. Put all the dry ingredients in a mortar and pound to a fine powder. Add the garlic and continue pounding to mix it in thoroughly.

Remove the wishbone and parson's nose from the ducks. Cut off the legs. Leave the breasts on the carcass and set them aside in the fridge. Rub the spiced salt into the duck legs, then cover and leave in the fridge overnight.

The next day, rub off the excess spiced salt from the duck legs. Warm duck or goose fat in a pan and immerse the duck legs. Cover and leave to cook very gently for 1½-2 hours. Meanwhile, prepare the other components of the dish.

Trim off the top of the leaves from the pak choi and cut off the stalk. Wash each pak choi and dry thoroughly, then season and fold each one over in half to make a neat parcel. Scatter the finely chopped garlic over a baking tray or dish. Arrange the pak choi parcels in the tray, then set aside until ready to cook.

For the sauce, cut one of the limes in half lengthways and squeeze out 1 tablespoon juice. Put this into a small saucepan and set aside. Peel the other half of the lime, as well as the other limes, and cut out the segments from between the membranes. Set the segments aside. Put the ginger in a bowl, pour over boiling water and drain; repeat two more times. Set the ginger aside with the lime segments.

Preheat the oven to 230°C/gas mark 8.

Heat a film of sunflower oil with a little duck or goose fat in a large cast-iron frying pan with an ovenproof handle. Season the duck breasts, then put them (still on the

Mallards, being wild, are very lean. This is a very successful way to prepare them. The initial idea came from Jane Grigson's pairing of mallard and pineapple, then was further inspired by a Japanese chef who worked with me at Fulham Road.

carcasses) into the pan, breast side down. Sear and brown for 2½ minutes, then turn the carcasses so you can sear and brown the 'crown' for a further 2 minutes. Transfer to the oven to finish cooking for about 15 minutes, then remove and set aside to rest in a warm place while you finish the other components.

Reduce the oven temperature to 170°C/gas mark 3. Put the pak choi into the oven and cook for 15 minutes. Check now and then to be sure the pak choi isn't browning – cover with foil if necessary.

Meanwhile, peel the pineapple and cut into 1 cm dice, discarding the core. Heat a dry frying pan, add the pineapple and sprinkle it with sugar. Cook over a moderately high heat, tossing the pineapple pieces constantly, to caramelize them on all sides. Transfer the pineapple to a plate and set aside.

Drain the duck legs on kitchen paper. Heat a heavy frying pan, put in the duck legs, skin side down, and cook until crisp and browned. Keep hot.

To finish the sauce, add the sugar to the lime juice in the small saucepan and bring up to the boil, swirling to dissolve the sugar. Cook until slightly caramelized, then add the juices from the resting duck breasts and the chicken or veal stock. Stir in the cornflour mixture and bring back to the boil, stirring, to thicken the sauce. Add the ginger and lime segments. Check the seasoning.

To serve, take the duck breasts off the carcasses. Put two baby pak choi parcels on each plate and set a duck breast on top. Toss the pineapple with the red chilli and dot round the pak choi. Rest a duck leg against the side of the pak choi, pointing up, and drizzle round the sauce.

Pan-roasted ox tongue with salad of green beans, shallots and rosemary oil

1 fresh ox tongue, prepared for
cooking by the butcher
butcher's brine (see Crisp-fried
crubeens, page 160)
vegetable stock, or water with
flavouring vegetables (roughly
chopped carrot, onion, leek
and celery) and bouquet garni
sunflower oil
Garlic confit (see page 132)

Serves 6

For the salad
6 sprigs of fresh rosemary
100 ml olive oil
1 teaspoon Dijon mustard
dash of white wine vinegar,
or more to taste
300 g fine green beans, trimmed
4 shallots, peeled and very finely diced
salt and freshly ground black pepper

Tongue has a soft texture which many people don't like – especially children – but slicing it and crisping it on the outside makes it very appealing. With the salad it makes a magical dish.

Put the tongue into the brine and cover with a plate to keep it submerged. Cover the bowl, then leave in the refrigerator for 2 days.

Drain the tongue (discard the brine). Put it into a saucepan and cover with vegetable stock, or with water, adding the flavouring vegetables and bouquet garni. Bring to the boil, then reduce the heat and simmer for 2½ hours or until the tongue is tender.

Lift out the tongue. Trim off the straggly ends and excess fat, and peel off the cardboard-like skin. Put the tongue into a bowl. Strain the cooking liquid into the bowl to cover the tongue and leave to cool.

To make the salad, pull the leaves from the rosemary stalks and grind them to a powder in a mortar and pestle. Put the oil, mustard and vinegar in a bowl and whisk together until emulsified. Add the powdered rosemary and stir well, then pass through a fine sieve. Season to taste.

Blanch the green beans in boiling salted water for 2-3 minutes or until just tender but still crisp. Drain and refresh in cold water. Set aside.

Drain the cold tongue and cut vertically into 1 cm slices. Dry on kitchen paper, then season the slices. Heat a film of oil in a heavy-based frying pan and brown the slices of tongue on both sides. Keep warm.

Dress the green beans with the rosemary vinaigrette and toss with the shallots. Serve the tongue with the salad and garlic confit.

Haunch of venison with pickled red cabbage

Serves 6

½ small haunch of venison, fillet end,
   seam boned (about 1.4 kg
   boned weight)
sunflower oil
good pinch of sugar
Pickled red cabbage (see page 204)
For the marinade
mirepoix of 100 g each diced carrot,
   celery and onion

3 garlic cloves, peeled and crushed
2 tablespoons sunflower oil
450 ml red wine
1 teaspoon black peppercorns
1 star anise
1 bay leaf
a few sprigs of fresh thyme
salt and freshly ground black pepper

To make the marinade, heat the oil in a large saucepan, add the mirepoix and garlic, and cook until softened but not brown. Add the remaining marinade ingredients and bring almost to the boil, then remove from the heat and cool.

Pour the marinade into a big bowl and add the pieces of venison. Cover and leave to marinate in the refrigerator for 12 hours.

Preheat the oven to 230°C/gas mark 8.

Remove the venison and dry well on kitchen paper. Heat a film of sunflower oil in a large heavy-based pan with an ovenproof handle. Add the venison and brown and sear on all sides. Transfer to the oven and roast for 10-20 minutes, according to the size of the pieces (for rare/medium rare meat). Remove from the oven, cover with foil and leave to rest for 10 minutes.

While the venison is being cooked, strain the marinade and pour it into a saucepan. Add the star anise from the sieve. Bring to the boil and reduce to 150 ml. Discard the star anise and stir in the sugar. Keep warm.

Reheat the cabbage.

Carve the pieces of venison against the grain. Add the juices to the reduced marinade, and check the seasoning. Drain the cabbage and pile in the centre of the plates. Top with the venison and serve with the gravy.

Seam boning – which takes all the meaty muscles individually from the bone – has become very popular in restaurant kitchens over the past 5-6 years. This is delicious with a celeriac and potato mash (see page 132) and chestnuts with sprouts and bacon (see page 180).

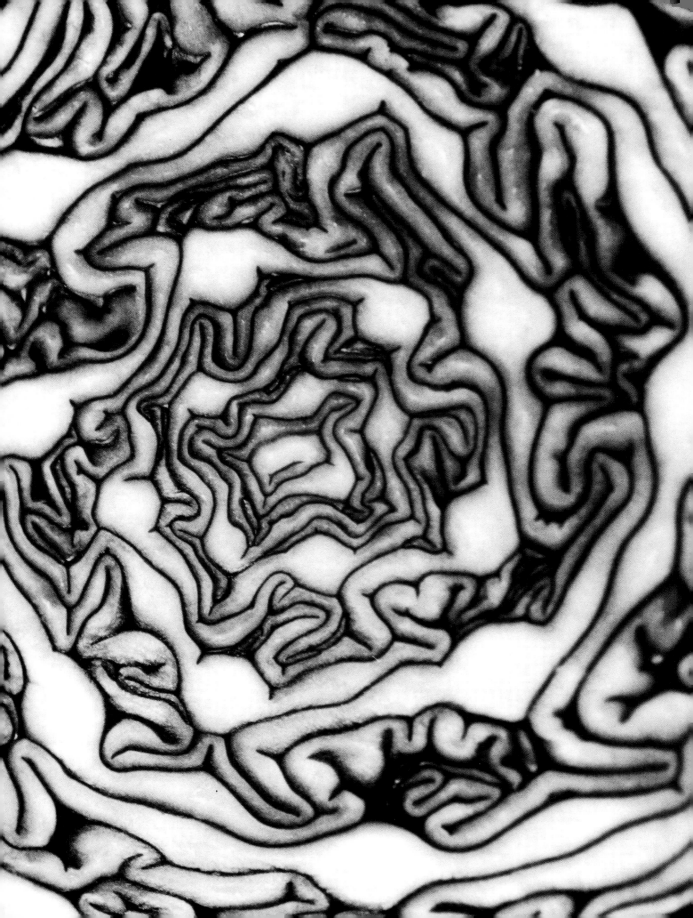

Rump of veal with leeks, girolles and truffle oil juice

Serves 4

1 joint rump of veal, seam boned
  (700–900 g)
sunflower oil
12 small leeks, about 1 cm in diameter
  and trimmed to 13 cm lengths
olive oil
50 g shallots, peeled and chopped

75 g fresh chanterelles (girolles),
  cleaned and broken up if large
2 tablespoons finely chopped mixed
  fresh chervil and chives
1 tablespoon truffle oil
coarse sea salt to finish
salt and freshly ground black pepper

Preheat the oven to 220°C/gas mark 7.

Season the pieces of veal. Heat a film of sunflower oil in a heavy-based pan (ideally one that can go into the oven). Add the pieces of veal and sear on all sides until browned. Transfer to the oven and roast for 35 minutes (the meat will be rosy-pink). Wrap the meat in foil and set aside to rest for 15 minutes.

Meanwhile, drop the leeks into a saucepan of boiling salted water and cook until almost tender. Drain and refresh. Split the leeks in half lengthways, then cut across in half. Set aside in a warm place.

Heat a film of olive oil in a pan and cook the shallots gently until softened. Turn up the heat slightly and add the chanterelles. Season with salt and pepper. Cook until the chanterelles start to exude their juices. Add the leeks and heat through. Stir in the herbs. Keep warm.

Unwrap the veal. Put the juices that have collected in the foil into a small pan with the truffle oil and season. If you have any veal stock, add a little of this too. Warm gently.

Carve the pieces of veal into 3 mm slices, cutting against the grain. Arrange on a heated platter. Place the leeks and chanterelles on the meat, and sprinkle with coarse sea salt. Spoon over the truffle oil juice and serve.

This is one of the few ways I use truffle oil. It has such a strong, powerful flavour that it can easily take over a dish. Ask your butcher to bone the veal for you – seam boning takes all the meaty muscles individually from the bone so you have nice pieces of meat to cook.

Brussels sprouts with chestnuts and bacon

Serves 4-6

75 g good unsmoked streaky bacon,
   cut into lardons
600 g small Brussels sprouts, trimmed
sunflower oil
400 g vacuum-packed cooked
   chestnuts
salt and freshly ground black pepper

Preheat the grill.

Spread out the bacon lardons on a baking tray or sheet of foil and grill until cooked, stirring occasionally.

Meanwhile, blanch the sprouts in a saucepan of boiling salted water for 2 minutes or until just tender. Drain and refresh. Set aside.

Heat a film of oil in a frying pan, add the chestnuts and cook gently to heat and colour on all sides. Add the sprouts and the bacon with all its fat and season to taste. Heat through, stirring, then serve.

This is the perfect accompaniment for game.

Swede purée with black pepper

Serves 4

700 g swede, peeled and
cut into chunks
100 g good unsmoked streaky bacon,
cut into lardons
salt and freshly ground black pepper

You can leave out the bacon here, and just enjoy the swede on its own, although I love the two flavours together.

If using the bacon, preheat the grill.

Cook the swede in a saucepan of boiling salted water for 15 minutes or until tender but not mushy.

Meanwhile, spread out the bacon lardons on a baking tray or sheet of foil and grill until cooked, stirring occasionally.

Drain the swede well and return it to the pan. Dry out over a very low heat for a minute or two, then hand mash with a potato masher or fork to a coarse purée. Season with salt and plenty of freshly ground black pepper. Serve hot, topped with the bacon and its fat.

Colcannon

Serves 4

500 g medium-sized floury potatoes
½ Savoy cabbage, cored and shredded
100 ml milk
60 g unsalted butter, plus extra
  for serving

2 spring onions, trimmed and chopped
  (white and some of the green)
salt and freshly ground black pepper
coarse sea salt to finish

Put the unpeeled potatoes into a pan of salted water, bring to the boil and simmer for 20-25 minutes or until tender. Drain and return to the empty pan, off the heat. Cover with a tea towel (or newspaper) and leave to steam and dry off for 5 minutes. Then uncover and leave until cool enough to handle.

Meanwhile, blanch the cabbage in boiling salted water until tender but still crisp. Drain well, then refresh briefly under cold running water. Chop the cabbage roughly to cut up the long strands.

Combine the milk, butter and spring onions in a saucepan and warm gently, without boiling, until the butter has melted (you want the spring onions to remain crunchy). Remove from the heat and keep warm.

Peel the potatoes and put them through a mouli-légumes or potato ricer into a clean saucepan. Add the milk mixture and beat with a wooden spoon to combine. Mix in the cabbage and reheat gently. Season with salt and pepper.

Put the colcannon into a warm bowl and place a few thin slices of butter on top. Sprinkle with a little coarse sea salt and serve immediately.

I remember someone trying to convince me that kale was the thing to use in Colcannon, which is a traditional Hallowe'en dish in Ireland. While it's true that there's loads of kale at this time of year – September, October – I'm not a great fan of it, and I like to serve Colcannon year round. I prefer the Savoy green cabbage, but either way, with cabbage or kale, it's a great dish.

Broccoli with anchovy butter

Serves 4

500 g broccoli
hazelnut oil to finish (optional)
For the anchovy butter
80 g unsalted butter, softened
3 anchovy fillets

1 tablespoon chopped fresh parsley
grated zest of 1 lemon
40 g hard goat's cheese, grated
freshly ground black pepper

Anchovy and goat's cheese go well together and are a perfect match for brassicas such as broccoli, giving a lift to what can be a very uninteresting vegetable.

First make the anchovy butter. Put the butter, anchovies, parsley and lemon zest in a food processor and blend until smooth. Add the goat's cheese and pepper to taste and blend again briefly just to mix, but not to make the mixture smooth again. Scrape out on to a sheet of greaseproof paper and shape into a neat log about 3 cm in diameter. Wrap up in the paper and chill until firm.

Cut the florets from the broccoli. Peel the stalks and cut them across into discs about 1 cm thick.

Drop the broccoli into a saucepan of boiling salted water and cook for 4–5 minutes or until just tender but still crisp. Drain and refresh, then turn into a hot serving dish. Thinly slice the anchovy butter into discs and lay over the hot broccoli. If the oven is on, put the dish in to heat briefly – this will help to melt the anchovy butter. If you like, sprinkle a tiny bit of hazelnut oil over the top, then serve.

Baked semolina with honeyed dates, Brittany sablés

Serves 8

600 ml full-cream milk
grated zest of 2 lemons
75 g caster sugar
50 g unsalted butter
130 g semolina
120 ml double cream
8 Brittany sablés (see page 205),
baked in discs the same diameter
as the semolina puddings

3 eggs, separated
8 sprigs of lamb's lettuce
For the honeyed dates
16 fresh dates
120 ml freshly squeezed lemon juice
2 tablespoons clear honey such
as acacia, or to taste
1 teaspoon arrowroot mixed with
1 teaspoon cold water

Lemon curd is delicious with this (see the recipe on page 140) – add it in small dollops between the dates on the serving plates. The semolina puddings can be made in advance and then reheated in the microwave.

First prepare the dates. Peel them, then cut into quarters lengthways and remove the stones. Put the dates in a bowl and set aside. Pour the lemon juice into a saucepan with honey to sweeten to taste and heat. Add the arrowroot mixture and bring to the boil, stirring until thickened. (The syrup will smell horrible when it is hot, but mellows out when cool.) Pour the hot syrup over the dates; it should almost cover them. Cool, then leave to macerate overnight.

The next day, make the semolina puddings. Pour the milk into a heavy-based saucepan and add the lemon zest. Heat until bubbles form round the edge, then remove from the heat and leave to infuse for 20 minutes.

Strain the milk and return to the pan. Add the sugar and butter and bring to the boil. Gradually add the semolina, raining it in as you do with polenta, stirring constantly (ideally have a whisk in one hand and a wooden spoon in the other so you can get into the corners of the pan). Reduce the heat to low and cook for 2 minutes, stirring. The mixture will be very thick. Remove from the heat and add the cream. When it has been mixed in, add the egg yolks and mix well. Leave to cool to room temperature.

Preheat the oven to 150°C/gas mark 2. Brush soft butter over the insides of 8 ramekins of 150 ml capacity, then coat lightly with caster sugar. Set aside.

Whisk the egg whites until stiff and fold into the semolina mixture. Spoon into the ramekins to fill them to the top. Wrap each ramekin in cling film, not stretching it tight, and prick the top with the tip of a knife so that steam can escape. Set the ramekins in a roasting tin of hot water (bain marie) and bake for 20-25 minutes or until just firm to the touch. Remove from the bain marie and peel off the cling film.

To serve, set a sablé in the centre of each plate. Loosen the semolina puddings with a knife, then turn them out of the ramekins on to the sablés. Arrange the date slivers round the puddings, criss-crossing them, and drizzle on some of the honey syrup. Dip the lamb's lettuce into the syrup and use to garnish the plates.

Clementine and pistachio compote with cardamom

Serves 4-6

700 g clementines

6 cardamom pods

170 g sugar

1 small bay leaf

50 g shelled pistachios, coarsely chopped
    (preferably Turkish)

lightly sweetened crème fraîche
    for serving

Using a citrus zester, take fine strips of zest from one of the clementines. Blanch the zest in boiling water for 1 minute, then drain well and set aside. Peel all the clementines, removing the filaments, then separate into segments. Set aside.

Warm the cardamom pods in a small dry pan just until you can smell their delicious spicy aroma. Tip them on to a cutting board and crack open the pods with the side of a large chef's knife. Scrape the tiny black seeds into a mortar and gently crush with the pestle just to break them up.

Put the sugar in a heavy-based saucepan with 450 ml water and bring to the boil, stirring to dissolve the sugar. Add the cardamom seeds and bay leaf and stir. Simmer for 5 minutes. Add the clementine segments and poach gently for 7-10 minutes.

Using a slotted spoon, remove the clementine segments from the syrup to a bowl and reserve. Boil the poaching syrup to reduce by half, then pour it over the clementines. Leave to cool, then chill well.

Discard the bay leaf before serving, sprinkled with the strips of clementine zest and pistachios. Serve with lightly sweetened crème fraîche.

Serve this with something chocolatey, such as the sorbet on page 146, the tuiles on page 205, or a chocolate cake or brownie.

Treacle tart

Serves 12

200 g plain flour

½ teaspoon salt

100 g chilled unsalted butter, cut
  into small pieces

1 egg yolk

For the filling

2 Granny Smith apples

grated zest and juice of 1 lemon

150 ml golden syrup

150 ml black treacle

300 ml whipping cream

6 eggs, lightly beaten

225 g fresh white breadcrumbs

Sift the flour and salt on to a work surface, preferably a marble slab. Make a well in the centre of the flour and put in the butter. Lightly beat the egg yolk with 3 tablespoons cold water and pour over the butter. Using your fingertips, work the egg yolk mixture into the butter, then gradually incorporate the flour. When the mixture has the consistency of coarse crumbs, gather it into a ball.

I can never understand why recipes for treacle tart contain no treacle. This one does, with some tart apple to cut through the richness of the other filling ingredients.

Very lightly flour the work surface. Knead and mix the dough by pushing it away from you with the heel of your hand and then gathering it up into a ball again. Continue this kneading for 1-2 minutes or until the dough is smooth. Shape into a ball again, wrap in cling film and chill for 30 minutes.

Preheat the oven to 190°C/gas mark 5.

Roll out the dough and use to line a deep 25 cm fluted tart tin with a removable base. Prick the bottom of the pastry case, then line it with greaseproof paper and fill with dried beans. Bake blind for about 15 minutes or until the pastry case is set. Remove and discard the paper and beans. Set the pastry case aside. Leave the oven on.

Peel and core the apples, then grate them into a bowl. Add the lemon zest and juice, and toss to coat all the apple. Put the syrup, treacle and cream in a saucepan and warm until bubbles start to form round the edge. Add to the apples together with the eggs and crumbs, and stir to mix. Pour into the pastry case.

Bake the tart for 30-40 minutes or until the filling is just set and the edge of the pastry case is golden brown. Leave to cool before serving.

Hot chocolate cake with Banyuls syrup

Serves 10

45 g unsalted butter

225 g dark chocolate, preferably Valrhona
or a good Belgian chocolate, chopped

3 eggs, separated + 3 egg whites

65 g caster sugar

For the ganache

50 g dark chocolate, preferably Valrhona
or a good Belgian chocolate, chopped

4 tablespoons double cream

For the Banyuls syrup

450 ml Banyuls wine

$4^{1}/_{2}$ teaspoons arrowroot mixed with
2 teaspoons water

To finish

icing sugar

cocoa powder

Preheat the oven to 180°C/gas mark 4. Brush a thin layer of melted butter all over the inside of 10 moulds of a deep muffin tray. Each mould should be about 7 cm diameter and 3 cm deep. Put into the fridge or freezer to chill until the butter has set. Brush with another layer of melted butter, then dust with flour and shake out excess. Set aside.

To make the ganache, bring the cream to the boil in a small saucepan, then slowly pour it over the chocolate and stir until melted. Leave to cool until cold but not set.

This is a great pudding for a party because the cakes can be prepared ahead of time, ready for baking, and kept in the fridge. If you don't want to bother making the ganache, you can use good chocolate truffles instead, cut in half.

For the cakes, put the butter and chocolate in a heavy-based saucepan and melt gently (or do this in the microwave). Remove from the heat and cool until lukewarm.

Meanwhile, whisk the 6 egg whites until frothy. Gradually whisk in one-third of the sugar and continue whisking until the meringue will hold a soft peak. Add another third of the sugar and whisk until the meringue is thick and glossy. Add the remaining sugar and whisk to a stiff peak. Add the yolks to the chocolate mixture and stir well; the mixture will become grainy. Fold in the meringue.

Half fill the prepared moulds with the chocolate mousse mixture and smooth the tops. Add a blob of ganache to the centre of each and spread out gently to 3-4 mm thickness. The ganache should not touch the side of the mould. Cover with the rest of the chocolate mousse mixture and smooth the tops level with the rim of the mould (a hot palette knife makes this easier). Bake for about 10 minutes. The cakes will rise like a soufflé and feel just firm to a light touch when done.

Meanwhile, to make the syrup, pour the wine into a saucepan. Add the arrowroot mixture and bring to the boil, stirring until thickened. Remove from the heat and keep hot.

Place a sheet of greaseproof paper over the muffin tray, then cover with an inverted large baking tray. Holding it all together, turn over so the cakes fall on to the paper-lined tray. Quickly set each cake, right way up, on a plate. Drizzle over and round the hot Banyuls syrup. Dust with sifted icing sugar and cocoa powder, and serve straight away.

Drunken fruits with poached pear and mascarpone

Serves 8

250 g sugar

4 ripe but firm pears

150 ml dark rum or brandy

500 g mixed dried fruits, such as
    prunes, apricots, figs and
    cranberries (not ready-to-eat)

To serve

250 g mascarpone

caster sugar

grated zest of 2 lemons

Put the sugar in a saucepan large enough to hold the pears comfortably. Add 1.5 litres of water and bring to the boil, stirring to dissolve the sugar. Peel the pears and add to the syrup; it should cover them completely. Simmer gently for about 20 minutes or until the pears are just tender – test with a skewer. Remove from the heat and leave to cool in the syrup.

When the pears are cool, remove them from the syrup with a slotted spoon and put into a deep bowl. Pour over enough syrup just to cover them, then cover and set aside.

Bring the remaining syrup back to the boil. Remove from the heat and stir in the rum or brandy. Pour this hot syrup over the dried fruits. Leave to rehydrate overnight.

The next day, drain the dried fruits, reserving the syrup, and remove the stones. Drain the pears and cut them in half; remove the cores neatly.

Sweeten the mascarpone to taste and stir in the lemon zest. Put a large spoonful of drunken fruits in the centre of each plate and top with a pear half. Drizzle over the reserved syrup. Add a small dollop or quenelle of mascarpone and serve.

Search out a good mascarpone from an Italian deli for this. You'll find that it is much less bland than the mascarpone sold in supermarkets. Serve with Brittany sablés (see page 205) or Cinnamon biscuits (see page 194), if you like.

Apple compote with cinnamon custard and cinnamon biscuits

Serves 6-8

6 Granny Smith apples

2 Bramleys apples

juice of 1 lemon

30 g unsalted butter

1/4 teaspoon ground cinnamon

caster sugar to taste

75 g sultanas, soaked in Calvados
   until plump

75 g coarsely chopped walnuts,
   preferably freshly shelled

For the cinnamon biscuits

120 g plain flour

60 g rice flour

pinch of salt

1 teaspoon ground cinnamon

120 g unsalted butter, at room
   temperature

45 g caster sugar + extra for sprinkling

1 egg yolk

For the cinnamon custard

250 ml milk

250 ml double cream

3 cinnamon sticks, broken into pieces

good pinch of ground cinnamon

5 egg yolks

60 g caster sugar

First make the cinnamon biscuits. Sift the flours with the salt and cinnamon. Cream the butter with the sugar until pale and fluffy. Beat in the egg yolk. Add the flour mixture and bring together with your hand, adding a few drops of water if necessary to help bind to a smooth dough. Wrap and chill for 20-30 minutes.

Preheat the oven to 180°C/gas mark 4.

Divide the dough in half and roll out each half thinly (to about 5 mm) on a surface sprinkled with caster sugar. Dust the dough with sugar as you roll it out. Cut out 8cm rounds and transfer to heavy baking sheets lined with non-stick liners. Bake for 10-15 minutes or until very lightly browned at the edge. The biscuits should still be a bit soft in the centre – take care not to overcook. Remove from the oven and cool for a few minutes on the baking sheets before transferring to wire racks to cool completely.

Using two varieties of apples is the secret here – the Bramleys will break down, while the Granny Smiths will be tender but still keep their shape.

To make the custard, pour the milk and cream into a heavy-based saucepan and add the cinnamon sticks and ground cinnamon. Heat until bubbles start to form round the edge of the pan, then remove from the heat and set aside to infuse for 20 minutes. Meanwhile, put the egg yolks and sugar in a heatproof bowl set over a pan of hot water and whisk until very thick and a pale lemon colour. Strain the hot milk mixture into the yolks, stirring to mix. Return the mixture to the saucepan. Set over a low heat and cook, stirring constantly, for about 10 minutes or until the custard thickens. You should be able to run your finger across the custard on the back of the spoon and leave a clear trail. Keep the custard hot.

Peel, core and roughly dice the apples, then sprinkle with the lemon juice and toss to coat. Melt the butter in a wide pan until foaming, then add the apples with the lemon juice and the cinnamon. Cook gently, stirring occasionally, for about 15 minutes. Add sugar to sweeten to taste and stir until dissolved. Add the sultanas and walnuts and warm through for a few minutes.

Pour the custard into soup plates and spoon the apple compote into the middle. Serve hot with the cinnamon biscuits.

Slow-cooked comfort food – stews, casseroles and daubes – demands comfort wine. Substance calls for substance. Winter is a time for fuelling up with meat, two root veg and potatoes, and red wines with plenty of (ripe) tannins help to digest and break down meat-and-starch combinations. As it says in the Bible, 'use a little wine for thy stomach's sake'. Now is the season for those reliable sun-burnished antique Riojas and Barolos, old-fashioned mahogany reds, or to experience the smooth, caramelized flavours conferred by age in the bottle of a white Rioja or an old Burgundy or Hunter Valley Semillon.

Another food and wine formula, such as it is, is relatively straightforward: if the central ingredient is wonderful and has a flavour that needs no dressing up, enjoy it with a great wine. A simple side of best beef asks for a great claret, lobster demands a Meursault or Puligny-Montrachet, venison gratefully soaks up great Rhones such as Cornas or Cote-Rotie. An Irish stew doesn't call for finesse, but rather power and savoury warmth by the bucket-load, so I would choose a so-called peasant wine, a gutsy Primitivo or a Cannonau from Southern Italy and Sardinia respectively. With wines like these you can smell and taste the sun-baked fruits of the Mediterranean wines during sunless winter days.

Douglas Wregg

Winter cheese

Amongst all the variations of cheesemaking, seasons have a part to play, because the cheese changes when the milk changes, and the milk changes when the animal's feed changes. However, seasons are only one of the factors influencing cheese quality. The type of milk used – cow's, ewe's or goat's – the weather, pasteurisation, the length of the ageing period and so on are also important factors, and every cheese gets individual attention from its maker.

Winter is the best time for many of the hard cheeses. Excellent cheddars are often made in the winter months when the cows are indoors on dry feed:

Cheddar
Cheshire
Lancashire
Caerphilly

On the whole the cheeses made at this time of year will be eaten a few months later (late winter to spring), except the cheddars which will be eaten the same time of year but the following year, when they are over a year old.

Randolph Hodgson, Neal's Yard Dairy

Basics

Bacon brioche

This is something I came up with when I was working at Fulham Road and wanted a bread to serve with the rump steak burger (see page 86).

Makes 1 loaf

sunflower oil

175 g unsmoked streaky bacon, rind removed and cut into small bits

1 small onion, peeled and very finely chopped

1½ teaspoons chopped fresh marjoram

225 g unsalted butter, at room temperature

3 large eggs

300 g strong white bread flour

pinch of salt

1 sachet easy-blend dried yeast (about 7 g)

about 2 tablespoons warm milk, if needed

1 small egg yolk lightly beaten with 1 teaspoon water

Heat a film of oil in a frying pan and sweat the bacon until it starts to brown. Add the onion and marjoram, and continue cooking until the onion is softened and the bacon is crisp. Tip on to kitchen paper and leave to drain and cool.

Put the butter in the bowl of a table-top electric mixer, or into a mixing bowl if using a hand-held mixer. Beat until soft and creamy. Beat in the eggs one by one. Sift the flour and salt and add to the bowl with the yeast. Beat thoroughly. If the dough seems too dry to come together, add the warm milk. The dough should be firm at this stage.

Fit the dough hook to the mixer, or turn the dough out on to a work surface. Knead until smooth and quite elastic. Add the bacon mixture and work into the dough until evenly distributed. Shape into a ball. Put into a clean bowl, cover with a cloth and leave at room temperature to rise until doubled in volume.

Knock back the dough on a lightly floured surface, then shape it into an oblong and place in a lightly oiled loaf tin of 1.3 litre capacity. The dough should half fill the tin. Cover and leave to rise at room temperature until the dough fills the tin.

Preheat the oven to 190°C/gas mark 5.

Brush the top of the loaf with the egg yolk mixture, then bake for about 30 minutes or until risen and golden brown. Test if the bread is done by tipping it out of the tin and tapping it gently on the base; it should sound hollow. Turn out on to a wire rack to cool.

Ham stock

Makes about 1.2 litres

1 onion, peeled

1 carrot, peeled

½ celery stick, trimmed

1 leek, trimmed

1 green gammon bone

any raw gammon skin or bacon rinds you may have

1 large fresh bouquet garni of parsley, thyme and bay leaf

5 black peppercorns

Cut the vegetables into large pieces and put into a pot with the remaining ingredients. Cover generously with about 2 litres cold water. Bring to the boil, skimming off the scum, then reduce the heat and simmer for 2 hours. Strain.

Dill bread

I use plain flour to make this yeasted bread, which is unusual, as is the inclusion of bicarbonate of soda as well as yeast, but it works perfectly. The bread is quite heavy because of the cheese. It is good with smoked salmon or spread with cream cheese.

Makes 1 loaf

$^1/_2$ small onion, peeled and finely chopped

15 g unsalted butter

570 g plain flour

1 teaspoon bicarbonate of soda

2 tablespoons caster sugar

1 teaspoon salt

1 sachet easy blend dried yeast (about 7 g)

1 bunch of fresh dill (about 15 g), roughly chopped

225 g cottage cheese

1 large egg, beaten

Sweat the onion gently in the butter until soft but not browned. Remove from the heat and leave to cool slightly.

Sift the flour, bicarbonate of soda, sugar and salt into a bowl. Add the yeast and dill, and stir to incorporate evenly. Add the softened onion, cottage cheese, egg and enough warm water to bind to a dough (about 200 ml). Turn on to a lightly floured surface and knead until quite smooth and elastic, which will take about 10 minutes.

Shape the dough and place in an oiled loaf tin that is about 1.7 litre capacity. Cover and leave in a warm place until risen to fill the tin.

Preheat the oven to 190°C/gas mark 5.

Bake the bread for 30-35 minutes. Because it is heavy, the normal test of turning the loaf out and tapping it on the base will not produce a drum-like sound. So test like a cake with a skewer inserted into the centre, to be sure it is cooked through and no longer moist.

Remove from the oven and leave to cool in the tin for 30 minutes, then turn out on to a wire rack. Cover with a damp tea towel and leave to cool completely.

Soda bread

This comes from my wife Maria's mother. It is one of the best soda breads I have ever eaten. Try it with smoked salmon.

Makes 2 round loaves

250 g plain wholemeal flour

125 g self-raising white flour

125 g pinhead oatmeal

60 g bran

30 g wheat germ

1 teaspoon salt

2 teaspoons bicarbonate of soda

2 tablespoons treacle

600 ml buttermilk

Preheat the oven to 170°C/gas mark 3.

Combine the flours, oatmeal, bran, wheat germ, salt and bicarbonate of soda in a bowl. Stir together to mix. Add the treacle and buttermilk and mix to get a moist dough.

Turn the dough out on to a well-floured surface and cut in half. Knead each piece of dough about 10 times until the surface is smooth, then shape the dough into a ball. Set the balls on a floured baking tray. Use a sharp knife to slash a deep cross-cut in the top of each.

Bake for about 50 minutes or until the bread sounds hollow when rapped on the base. Cool on a wire rack. Eat while still really fresh.

Vanilla ice-cream

4 servings alone or 8 servings with a pudding

250 ml full-cream milk

250 ml double cream

1 vanilla pod, split open

6 egg yolks

100 g caster sugar

Pour the milk and cream into a heavy-based saucepan. Scrape the tiny seeds out of the vanilla pod into the milk, then add the pod too. Heat until bubbles start to form round the edge of the pan. Meanwhile, put the egg yolks and sugar in a heatproof bowl set over a pan of hot water and whisk until very thick and a pale lemon colour. Pour the hot milk mixture into the yolks, stirring to mix. Return the mixture to the rinsed-out saucepan. Set over a low heat and cook, stirring constantly, for about 10 minutes or until thickened – you should be able to run your finger across the custard on the back of the spoon and leave a clear trail. Do not allow the custard to boil. Remove from the heat and allow to cool, then chill until very cold.

Strain the cold custard. Pour into an ice-cream machine and freeze. Once softly frozen, transfer the ice-cream to a freezerproof container and put into the freezer to 'mature' for an hour or so. If freezing for longer than 1 hour, transfer the ice-cream to the fridge 20 minutes before serving to soften slightly.

For spiced bread ice-cream, omit the vanilla pod. Lay 2 thin slices (100 g) of spiced bread (see page 49) on a rack and leave to dry out overnight. Put the dry sponge slices in a food processor and process to coarse crumbs. When the ice-cream is thick, but has not yet finished freezing, add the spiced breadcrumbs.

Crème anglaise

If serving this with a pudding such as treacle tart (see recipe on page 188), make it with milk.

Makes 500 ml to serve 4–6

500 ml milk, or half milk and half double cream

1 vanilla pod, split open

5 egg yolks

60 g caster sugar

Pour the milk, or milk and cream, into a heavy-based saucepan. Scrape the tiny seeds out of the vanilla pod into the milk, then add the pod too. Heat until bubbles start to form round the edge of the pan, then remove from the heat and set aside to infuse for 20 minutes.

Meanwhile, put the egg yolks and sugar in a heatproof bowl set over a pan of hot water and whisk until thick and a pale lemon colour.

Remove the vanilla pod from the hot milk mixture, then pour into the yolks, stirring to mix. Return the mixture to the saucepan. Set over a low heat and cook, stirring constantly, for about 10 minutes or until the custard thickens. You should be able to run your finger across the custard on the back of the spoon and leave a clear trail. Serve hot or allow to cool completely and then chill.

Black pudding

The variations on black pudding are countless – in the north of England it is spicier and in France it is softer in texture and the fat doesn't show. Oatmeal is prominent in Irish puddings, and the Irish herb tansy is a traditional flavouring. I think black pudding should retain the piggy flavour and not be over-spiced, as it is always served as an accompaniment to something else. I don't expect that anyone will make this, but I include the recipe here for interest.

300 g streaky bacon, cut into 5 mm dice
sunflower oil
1 onion, peeled and finely chopped
good pinch of chopped fresh tansy (optional)
150 g lardo (the fat from Parma ham), cut into 5 mm dice
900 ml fresh pig's blood
250 g pinhead oatmeal
120 ml double cream
grated zest of $1/2$ lemon
good pinch of cayenne pepper
pig's intestines

Fry the bacon in a frying pan without any fat until golden brown, then tip into a colander set in a bowl to drain. Heat a film of sunflower oil in the pan and soften the onion without browning. Add the tansy and stir, then tip the onion into the colander with bacon.

Add the lardo to the hot pan, and toss and stir until it starts to exude its fat. Tip into the colander.

Warm the blood gently in a heavy saucepan, bringing it to room temperature, but taking care not to boil. Add the oatmeal and all the ingredients from the colander. Add the cream, lemon zest and cayenne, and stir to mix. Cook over a low heat for about 35 minutes, stirring constantly. Never approach boiling point. The oatmeal will expand, and the mixture will take on a firm consistency. Remove from the heat when it starts to thicken.

Put into a piping bag fitted with a large plain nozzle and pipe into the pig's intestines. Twist and cut 15 cm lengths.

Immerse the sausages in a pot of cold water and bring to the boil. As the sausages rise to the surface they will expand, and must then be pricked or they will burst. Handle them gently as they are delicate. Remove and lay them on a clean kitchen cloth. Leave to dry, uncovered, in a cold place such as the fridge for a day or two. (They will keep in the fridge for 3-4 days.)

To use, slice them and fry gently in a non-stick pan without any oil.

Oatcakes

Delicious with cheese.

Makes about 26
120 g medium oatmeal
120 g plain flour
60 g unsalted butter
1 tablespoon duck fat
1 teaspoon salt

Preheat the oven to 190°C/gas mark 5.

Put all the ingredients into a food processor and blend together, adding about 2 tablespoons cold water or just enough to bind the ingredients to a firm dough.

Roll out very thinly on a lightly floured surface and cut out 7 cm rounds or other shapes. Transfer to baking sheets lined with greaseproof paper and bake for 15-20 minutes or until just coloured. Cool on the baking sheets.

Pickled red cabbage

These pickled cabbages are delicious with almost anything, but particularly game, sausages and ham. They keep well in the fridge – 2-3 weeks in an airtight container – and can only get better the longer they are in the pickle.

Makes 1.2 kg to serve about 12

1 large red cabbage (about 1 kg), cored and finely shredded

coarse rock salt

For the brine

1 litre red wine

250 ml red wine vinegar

250 ml Cabernet Sauvignon vinegar

90 g sugar

$\frac{1}{2}$ star anise

$\frac{1}{2}$ cinnamon stick

6 cardamom pods

10 black peppercorns

$\frac{1}{4}$ teaspoon coriander seeds

$\frac{1}{4}$ teaspoon fennel seeds

4 juniper berries

$\frac{1}{2}$ nutmeg, grated

2 sprigs of fresh thyme

1 bay leaf

3 garlic cloves, peeled and crushed

Toss the shredded cabbage with coarse salt in a big bowl. Cover and leave in a cool place or the fridge overnight. The cabbage will go limp. Rinse well and drain.

To make the brine, put the wine, vinegars and sugar in a large saucepan (enamel-lined, aluminium or stainless steel) and bring to the boil, stirring occasionally to dissolve the sugar. Tie all the remaining ingredients in a piece of muslin and add to the pan. Add the cabbage and stir, then leave to simmer gently for 30 minutes. Remove from the heat and leave to cool.

Pour into a bowl or other container, cover and keep in the fridge. Remove the cabbage with tongs as you want it, and serve cold or reheat.

For pickled white cabbage, core and finely shred 1 large white or green cabbage, then toss with coarse salt and leave in a bowl in the fridge for 4 days or up to a week, stirring and turning occasionally. Rinse thoroughly and drain. Make the brine as above, using white wine instead of red, and white wine vinegar instead of the two red wine vinegars. Add the cabbage and simmer for just 15 minutes. Keep in the fridge as for pickled red cabbage.

Cheddar and cayenne sablés

We serve these tiny savoury biscuits with pre-dinner drinks.

Makes about 80 tiny rounds or fewer larger shapes

120 g plain flour

$\frac{1}{2}$ teaspoon salt

$\frac{1}{4}$ teaspoon cayenne pepper

120 g cold unsalted butter, diced

120 g mature Cheddar cheese, finely grated

1 egg yolk beaten with 1 teaspoon cold water

Put the flour, salt and cayenne in a food processor and pulse briefly to blend. Add the butter and process to make crumbs. Add the cheese and process just until the ingredients come together. Turn out on to a sheet of greaseproof paper and gather into a ball. Wrap and chill for at least 1 hour or, preferably, overnight.

Preheat the oven to 190°C/gas mark 5.

Roll out the dough on a lightly floured surface to about 3 mm thickness. Cut out rounds or other shapes (we cut 3 cm rounds in the restaurant) and place on baking sheets lined with non-stick silicone paper. Brush the biscuits with the egg yolk wash, then bake for 5 minutes or until shiny and golden brown all over. Cool on the baking sheets (the sablés are fragile).

Wholemeal tuiles

Makes about 28

75 g unsalted butter

125 g caster sugar

4 egg whites

75 g plain wholemeal flour

Melt the butter and cool to lukewarm. Mix with all the other ingredients, stirring until the sugar has dissolved, then cover and chill overnight.

The next day, preheat the oven to 180°C/gas mark 4. Make a template out of card if you want flat, shaped biscuits. rather than the traditional curved roof-tile shape. We make flat leaf shapes about 8 cm long. Line a baking sheet with non-stick silicone paper. (Bake only one sheet at a time if you want curved shapes, as the biscuits harden quickly once they are out of the oven.)

If using a template, set it on the baking sheet. Spoon the mixture inside the cut-out shape and spread it very thinly, right to the edges, then carefully lift off the template. Shape a few more biscuits on the sheet in the same way. For a roof-tile, put a teaspoonful of the mixture on the baking sheet, then spread out as thinly as possible with the back of the spoon to a round or oval shape.

Bake for 5-8 minutes or until the biscuits are slightly golden brown at the edges. Remove them immediately from the baking sheet; they will be fragile. Put flat shapes on a wire rack; drape the rounds or ovals for roof-tiles over a rolling pin. Leave to cool.

For chocolate tuiles, use 120 g plain flour and 30 g cocoa powder instead of the wholemeal flour. This is a much thicker mixture, so you need only about ½ teaspoon for each tuile, and the recipe will make about 75 (cut the quantities in half, if you wish).

Brittany sablés

This is a French equivalent of shortbread, rich and crumbly.

Makes about 36

300 g plain flour

1 tablespoon baking powder

½ teaspoon salt

100 g unsalted butter, at room temperature

200 g caster sugar

6 egg yolks

Sift the flour with the baking powder and salt. Using an electric mixer fitted with the dough hook cream the butter with the sugar until pale and fluffy. Add the egg yolks and beat them in, then add the flour and mix just until it comes together into a soft dough. Take care not to overmix or knead.

Cover the bowl and put into the fridge. Leave the dough to rest for at least 1 hour to firm up.

Preheat the oven to 170°C/gas mark 3.

Roll out the dough on a lightly floured surface to about 3 mm thickness. Cut out 7 cm discs or other shapes. If making sablés to accompany the semolina puddings on page 185, use the ramekins as a guide for cutting. Transfer to a baking sheet lined with non-stick silicone paper. Bake for 10-15 minutes or until a pale golden brown. The biscuits should still be slightly soft in the centre.

Transfer to a wire rack to cool. The biscuits will become brittle quite quickly. They can be kept for 2-3 days, stored in an airtight tin.

Weights and Measures

All recipes have been tested using metric weights and measures, and a standard non-convection oven.

1 teaspoon = 5 ml, 1 tablespoon = 15 ml. Spoons are measured level.

If you prefer to use imperial weights and measures, you can use the following table as a guide. However, note that conversions suggested here are not exact equivalents, and that metric and imperial measurements cannot be used together in the same recipe.

Weights		**Volume measures**		**Linear measures**	
15 g	(½ oz)	75 ml	(2½ fl oz)	3 mm	(⅛ in)
30 g	(1 oz)	90 ml	(3 fl oz)	5 mm	(¼ in)
55 g	(2 oz)	100 ml	(3½ fl oz)	1 cm	(½ in)
85 g	(3 oz)	120 ml	(4 fl oz)	2 cm	(¾ in)
100 g	(3½ oz)	150 ml	(5 fl oz)	2.5 cm	(1 in)
115 g	(4 oz)	200 ml	(7 fl oz)	5 cm	(2 in)
140 g	(5 oz)	250 ml	(8½ fl oz)	7.5 cm	(3 in)
170 g	(6 oz)	300 ml	(10 fl oz)	10 cm	(4 in)
200 g	(7 oz)	360 ml	(12 fl oz)	15 cm	(6 in)
225 g	(8 oz)	400 ml	(14 fl oz)	20 cm	(8 in)
300 g	(10½ oz)	450 ml	(15 fl oz)	25 cm	(10 in)
340 g	(12 oz)	500 ml	(17 fl oz)	30 cm	(12 in)
400 g	(14 oz)	600 ml	(1 pint)		
450 g	(1 lb)	750 ml	(1¼ pints)		
500 g	(1 lb 2 oz)	900 ml	(1½ pints)		
550 g	(1¼ lb)	1 litre	(1¾ pints)		
600 g	(1 lb 5 oz)	1.2 litres	(2 pints)		
675 g	(1½ lb)	1.5 litres	(2¾ pints)		
750 g	(1 lb 10 oz)	2 litres	(3½ pints)		
800 g	(1¾ lb)				
900 g	(2 lb)				
1 kg	(2¼ lb)				
1.25 kg	(2¾ lb)				
1.5 kg	(3 lb 3 oz)				
2 kg	(4½ lb)				

Index